Making Molehills
OUT OF
Mountains

Making Molehills OUT OF Mountains

**Reclaiming Your Personal Power
in Your Relationships**

Dr. Steve Frisch, Psy.D.

ALIVE & WELL PUBLICATIONS
CHICAGO, ILLINOIS

Copyright 1998 Steve Frisch, Psy.D. Printed and bound in the United States of America. All rights reserved. No part of this book may be reproduced or transmitted in any form or by any means, electronic or mechanical, including photocopying, recording, or by an information storage and retrieval system—except by a magazine or newspaper reviewer who may quote brief passages—without written permission from the publisher. For information, please contact Alive And Well Publications, 1330 N. Dearborn, Suite 1205, Chicago, Illinois 60610, (773) 477-8959. First printing 1998.

Although the author and publisher have made every effort to ensure the accuracy and completeness of information contained in this book, we assume no responsibility for errors, inaccuracies, omissions, or any inconsistency herein. Any slights of people, places, or organizations are unintentional.

Book cover and text design by Mary J. Burroughs.

Publisher's Cataloging in Publication

Frisch, Steve.
  Making molehills out of mountains: reclaiming your personal power in your relationships / Steve Frisch.--1st ed.
  p. cm.
  Preassigned LCCN: 97-94373
  ISBN 0-9651511-5-8

  1. Interpersonal conflict. 2. Forgiveness. I. Title.

BF637.I48F75 1998   158.2
                         QBI97-41098

For years I have been the collector of a wide variety of quotations. In preparing this book I have spent countless hours attempting to locate the origins of some of the quotations cited. If you know the names of sources that have been mistakenly overlooked, please contact the publisher at (773) 477-8959. My apologies to the authors, and to the readers for any inadvertent oversight of proper credit.

ATTENTION ORGANIZATIONS, CORPORATIONS, HEALING CENTERS, AND SCHOOLS OF SPIRITUAL DEVELOPMENT: Quantity discounts are available on bulk purchases of this book for educational purposes, fund raising, or gift giving. Special books, booklets, or book excerpts can be created to fit specific needs for promotion of your organizational missions. For information, please contact Alive And Well Publications, 1330 N. Dearborn Suite 1205, Chicago, IL 60610 or call (773) 477-8959.

Table of Contents

xiv   About the Author

xvii   About the Bridge-Building Program

2   What's it all about...

9   Part One: Reclaiming Your Personal Power

33   Part Two: Pinpointing the Issue

77   Part Three: Acceptance

121   Part Four: Unmet Emotional Needs

167 Part Five: Appreciation

193 Part Six: Power and Control

227 Part Seven: Making Molehills Out of Mountains

Acknowledgments

One more time my creative team has demonstrated how commitment to one's vision can create a miracle. Thank you for bringing your best efforts to bear on the completion of this project.

To my editor, Donna. You continue to teach me the subtleties of communicating with the written word. I greatly appreciate the effort you have invested in helping me polish my message into a readable form. Thank you!

To Mary Burroughs, our publication designer and creative director, you're like a fine wine. You keep getting better with each project. Once again, thanks for keeping the dream alive!

This book is one more opportunity for me to share with you the lessons I have learned from a collection of very special people. I have been blessed by the touch of so many who have provided me with yet another piece to the puzzle of life.

Again I take pause to acknowledge the gratitude I feel for the teachers in my life. You have come in all shapes and sizes, but it is your essence that lives within me. Thank you all so very, very much!

Dedication

In loving memory of my dearest friend, Jenny.
You taught me that being loved was more important
than being right. I am a better person today for having
known you. I feel blessed to have experienced your love,
though for much too short of a time. The essence of
who you were will live forever in my heart.

About the Author

Dr. Frisch is a clinical psychologist in private practice in Chicago, Illinois. He is a graduate of the Adler School of Professional Psychology where he received his doctorate in clinical psychology. He received his Masters Degree from the National College of Education where he specialized in addictions counseling. His undergraduate degree was awarded to him by the University of Cincinnati, where he graduated with honors.

Dr. Frisch received post-doctoral training in two specialties at the Adler School of Professional Psychology. He completed a certificate training program in clinical hypnosis at the Center For The Advanced Study Of Clinical Hypnosis. He also completed a certificate training program in marriage and family counseling. He is licensed by the state of Illinois as a clinical psychologist. He is certified in Illinois by IAODAPCA as a certified drug and alcohol counselor.

Dr. Frisch's first book, *The Comparative Effectiveness of Group Therapy Versus Individual Therapy As Measured By Self-Concept, Interpersonal Orientation, and Degree of Emotional Adjustment* was an empirical investigation of the treatment modalities he utilizes in his private practice. This book was based on a study he conducted to demonstrate the effectiveness of his treatment protocols.

He has since written the *Bridge-Builders* series, which focuses on the development and enrichment of relationships. As well, he has written the *Pathfinders* series, which focuses on personal growth and self-actualization.

His treatment philosophy has grown out of his diverse clinical background in which he has worked with a variety of different clinical populations. From these diverse experiences, Dr. Frisch has assimilated a variety of assessment and treatment interventions into his integrated treatment philosophy.

Dr. Frisch has worked on the staff of both inpatient and outpatient chemical dependency programs. This experience provided the foundation for his work with issues that arise from the impact of chemical dependency on the individual, the family, and the workplace.

As a result of his work in the field of chemical dependency, Dr. Frisch founded the Adult Children Institute. This treatment clinic specialized in working with adults who were raised in families that were emotionally organized around the influences of drugs and alcohol, sexual and physical abuse, and emotional neglect.

The Adult Children Institute developed treatment interventions that enabled the program's participants to develop effective ways to heal from the aftereffects of trauma they experienced from their earlier development. These aftereffects included substance abuse, depression, anxiety, low self-esteem, shame, and relationship issues such as fear of emotional intimacy and commitment.

Dr. Frisch co-developed and was the coordinator of a mental health program for homeless adults who required treatment for substance abuse and emotional disorders. He developed an individualized assessment and treatment protocol that provided the impetus and support for each individual to rebuild their lives within their local communities.

The Relationship Bridge Building and Pathfinders personal growth programs represent the integration of Dr. Frisch's ongoing research and work in the area of human growth and potential development. Program participants develop the necessary awareness and skills to create an empowered life that maximizes their full potential for both their interpersonal and professional lives.

Whether by individual consultation, group experiences, workshops, or seminars, Dr. Frisch engages his audiences with a mixture of common sense and sound psychological principles of change to awaken and inspire their dormant potential. He consults with individuals, couples, groups, and organizations that are seeking to implement the principles of development, change, and growth in their lives.

About the
Bridge-Building Program

The essential ingredient for a life full of wellness and purpose is our emotional and spiritual well-being. Our emotional and spiritual well-being is predicated upon the quality of the relationships we have with ourselves and with the people in our life.

Because of the connection between the quality of our significant relationships and our emotional and spiritual well-being, I created the Relationship Bridge-Building tenets. The Relationship Bridge-Building program was created from three fundamental premises. The first premise is that our life's journey is most fulfilling when we are able to create fulfilling relationships with the people who matter most. Very simply, the heart and soul of our emotional and spiritual well-being is closely linked to our ability to successfully navigate the oftentimes choppy waters of our interpersonal life.

The second premise of Relationship Bridge-Building is that our emotional and spiritual well-being is directly connected to the relationship we have with ourselves. Not one of us is immune from the toxic aspects of the relationship we create with ourselves. Yet, by healing the most fundamental of all relationships we maintain, the relationship with ourselves, we can be more open to creating a place in our world that honors us.

The third premise is that there is a set of skills easily learned that can enable anybody to repair the wounds we carry within us. Also, there is a set of skills we can easily learn that will enable us to create emotionally safe and satisfying relationships with people we choose to build relationship-bridges with.

Quite simply, we all are pursuing the same end—to create a life for ourselves based upon who we are as well as who we are fully capable of becoming. No matter where we are in our life's journey, we are always in the process of becoming. Yet oftentimes, we get stuck along the way. When we become stuck, we can often see that the root of our obstacles lies within our relationship with ourselves and the people in our lives.

When we become stuck, we can feel overwhelmed by an inherent sense of powerlessness. And there's a very good reason for that. What we all must eventually discover for ourselves is that we become stuck for one very simple reason—that reason being ourselves. And it's impossible to transcend ourselves without doing things differently than we have up to that point.

That really is the first step we all must take before we can ever transform the drama in our lives into a space of emotional and spiritual fulfillment. We need to discover one essential, inescapable truth—we are the sole creators of what our life is today. We need to better understand how we are not mere victims of other people's cruelty and hostility—rather that we are the author of all that exists in our life.

That is exactly what rises to the surface for participants in the Relationship Bridge-Building program. Responsibility and personal freedom are the core of what each participant discovers. It is through one's ability to create relationships with other people based upon mutual responsibility and personal freedom that unlocks each individual's emotional and spiritual prison. The prison created by blaming others for not meeting their responsibility to make and keep us happy.

Afterall, we all are searching for a way to create a space in our lives that brings honor to who we are. A space where the relationships we create nurture our growth and development. A space where the relationship we have with ourselves encourages us to experiment and play. A space where we find a way of reclaiming all of those disowned parts of ourselves and bring them back into our life.

As a personal growth program, Relationship Bridge-Building serves as a catalyst for transforming our life's journey. Quite simply, the only way to prepare for our life's journey is to begin the journey. And for many of us, the present moment is a tremendous amount of inertia to overcome.

This is exactly the point of Relationship Bridge-Building. To discover deep within ourselves the majesty of living life in the here-and-now. To discover how the present moment is a powerful goddess. To discover the skills that live within each and every one of ourselves that enables us to most fully live our lives in the present, in the cleanest way possible with the people who matter most.

Relationship Bridge-Building is a powerful elixir for what we all encounter in our lives from time to time: discouragement; cynicism; hopelessness; loneliness.

Just how might that be so? You see, the most important tenet of Relationship Bridge-Building is that we can stop defining ourselves by where we are in our lives today, for it is not so much where we are today, but in what direction our journey is moving us. And as we begin to feel more comfortable with our ability to create fulfilling relationships, we will discover a completely different direction to our journey.

That is the exact connection between the quality of our relationships and our emotional and spiritual well-being. For our relationships add a whole new dimension to our life's journey. Our relationships add a hue of meaning and purpose without which we become disconnected from our path, aimlessly cut adrift from our true purpose in life.

Developing the inherent skills to activate the dormant potential of cooperative living with the people who matter most is the ultimate aim of Relationship Bridge-Building. Anyone can soon discover the power that effective communication can have on their journey. Developing safe supportive relationships that build trust amongst people can truly liberate us from the pain that we experience when we feel overwhelmed by the *stuck* points in our relationships.

Discovering, perhaps for the first time, the power of acceptance as well as the immediate shift that acceptance brings to any of our relationships, is a truly empowering discovery. Discovering the capacity for acceptance within and how to bring it to our relationships will free us from the toxic effects that our own judgmentalness exerts upon our relationships.

As you acquaint yourself with Relationship Bridge-Building, you will see yourself reflected within the pages of this book. The words on each page will take on a very personal meaning to you—a meaning meant to awaken your soul to the possibilities of what your relationships can be.

As the tiny seeds of hope and potential within you are activated, be ready for what your life will become. For your life will become a wondrous mixture of hope and fear, growth and paralysis, excitement and discouragement.

And that's as it should be. But over time, the roller coaster ride will even out for you–of that you can be sure. And as it does, you will have trouble recognizing who is staring back at you as you look in the mirror everyday.

Let me share this one last thought with you as you begin your journey. We have a saying that describes people's experience in the Relationship Bridge-Building groups.

"You couldn't pay me a million dollars to do it again, but you couldn't pay me ten million dollars to have never done it at all."

It is with this spirit that I encourage you to launch your own search for the path that will [re]connect you to your life's journey.

I want to love you without clutching,
Appreciate you without judging.

Join you without invading,
Invite you without demanding.

Leave you without guilt.

Criticize you without blaming
and help you without insulting.

If I can have the same from you
then we can truly meet and
enrich each other.

-Virginia Satir

What's it all about ...

John Ruskin once said, "When love and skill work together, expect a masterpiece." Indeed, the most fundamental premise of the *Bridge-Builder's* series is that specific relationship skills combined with the willingness to apply them in a consistent, respectful fashion can transform any of your relationships into richly rewarding experiences.

The most important relationship skill is learning how to resolve the inevitable conflict that develops between two people. Its importance is easy enough to understand. We're all experts at *creating* conflict yet very few of us are as skilled at effectively *resolving* conflict.

There are many reasons that this fact is so. Some of us are so deathly afraid of another person's anger that we back down from escalating conflict, believing that if we just ignore the unresolved issues in our relationships things will get better. For others, we believe that if we confront a person with our anger and hurt feelings, we will be abandoned by that person. Yet others feel like their expressed feelings fall upon deaf ears, feeling defeated before they try to resolve an issue with their partner.

There are those of us who are merely misguided in our attempts to resolve conflict. We mistakenly believe that if we *fix* a person or a problem, things will magically revert to peaceful bliss. Still others believe the secret to resolving conflict is being well intended. For those individuals, good intentions, justifiable actions, and unfailing logic are ingredients of a formula that perpetuates hurt and resentment rather than mends the wounds caused by unresolved issues in their relationships.

No matter what the reasons are that we shy away from resolving conflict, the consequences are always the same. We surrender our personal power to our fears. We give away the control we possess to impact the well-being of our relationships. By shying away from resolving the relationship issues that exist between two people, we sabotage our best efforts to enrich our lives by building better bridges with the people who matter most. Worst of all, we undermine our emotional and spiritual well-being.

However, it doesn't have to remain that way. There's a way for you to reclaim your personal power. By mastering some very simple relationship skills, you'll rediscover the voice of empowerment that lives within you.

As you read *Making Molehills Out of Mountains,* you'll unearth nuggets of wisdom about yourself and your partner that will free you from the bonds of unresolved conflict. More than a self-help book, *Making Molehills Out of Mountains* is a blueprint for reclaiming your personal power by resolving conflict and healing open wounds.

You'll discover a new way to think about what conflict means between two people. More importantly, you'll learn how to resolve conflict. Beyond learning many new relationship skills, you'll begin to understand more clearly who you are. You'll learn that there's much more going on beneath the surface of your day to day disagreements with others than meets the eye.

By better understanding what those issues might be, you'll better be able to extinguish these disagreements before they take on a life of their own. The skills you'll learn in *Making Molehills Out of Mountains* will enhance your ability to communicate with your partner. Enhanced communication can only mean less disagreements, fewer hurt feelings, and a reduced number of conflicts that remain unresolved.

Although there are many important relationship skills discussed throughout this book, *Making Molehills Out of Mountains* focuses primarily on an important relationship skill I call *pinpointing the issue*. You'll learn what this skill is, how to identify the two elements of a conflict, and the specific steps used to apply this skill. Examples of other relationship skills to be discussed are empathy, validation, checking-in, self-disclosure, and much more.

The book is divided into seven parts. Each part contains a few chapters that will discuss an important facet of the process of making molehills out of mountains. Parts two through seven contain a familiar feature from my previous relationship book, *Bridge-Builder's Tips*. These are concrete suggestions that will help you focus your efforts on a specific aspect of the process of making molehills out of mountains. Here's a quick overview of each section.

Reclaiming Your Personal Power is an overview of the problems inherent in any relationship and the solution that can transform those problems. You will be asked to reflect upon and record the benefits derived from creating such a transformation.

Pinpointing the Issue is the section in which I discuss the importance of identifying the two levels of most conflicts—the *circumstance* and the *underlying relationship issue*. You'll learn how to identify those two elements so that you can make the best choice about how to problem-solve with your partner. This section sets the stage for the next four sections that discuss the themes that may exist in the underlying issues of your unresolved conflicts.

Acceptance, the following section, is the first theme of an underlying relationship issue I will discuss with you. You'll learn how the issue may appear in your relationship, the ways in which you may make your partner feel unaccepted, and how to remediate the situation. You'll learn two relationship skills—empathy and validation. When utilized, these two skills will leave your partner feeling accepted and your relationship more harmonious.

Unmet Emotional Needs is the second theme for an underlying relationship issue that I discuss. I identify two important emotional needs—secure connection and emotional safety—that we all need fulfilled in order to create close connections. This section focuses on the skills I call checking-in and self-disclosure. I also present to you two *Bridge-Builder's Tools* that will enable you to more easily meet your partner's emotional needs.

Appreciation is the third underlying relationship issue I discuss. This section challenges you to think about this dynamic as an important stabilizing influence in any relationship. You'll quickly see for yourself how the presence of appreciation for your partner alleviates conflict, while the absence of appreciation can quickly destabilize a relationship. I discuss two *Bridge-Builder's Tools* that will enable you to immediately transform judgment into appreciation, thus eliminating much conflict in your relationships.

Power and Control is the last theme for underlying relationship issues that I discuss. This section focuses on two specific aspects of this multi-dimensional dynamic—fear of intimacy and fear of loss of autonomy. In this section, you'll have an opportunity to examine how those two dynamics live and breathe in your relationships. More importantly, you'll examine what impact they have upon your relationships.

Making Molehills Out of Mountains is the last section of the book. In this section, I tie together all of the previous sections and I provide a blueprint for you to create your own personal style as to how to pinpoint the issue. The first chapter in this section has three separate *Bridge-Builder's Tips* that outline the specific steps for pinpointing the issue. The second chapter of this section contains five *Bridge-Builder's Tools* to assist you in executing the various relationship skills I have discussed with you throughout the book.

Making molehills out of mountains is a process you'll grow into over time. Although there are important concepts that you can learn in this book, the process itself can only be mastered through practice and patience. I promise you that there's light at the end of the tunnel, but you must walk through the darkness, as well.

As you learn to walk the walk, you'll learn many things about yourself that will serve to empower you in your life's journey. You'll also have the opportunity to identify specific behaviors that create problems for you rather than honor you. You'll always have the option to discard those behaviors as you create new ways of thinking, acting, and feeling.

Whatever your experiences are, please know that what you learn throughout your journey in this book can profoundly change the way you build relationship bridges with the people who matter most. I know full well that these changes will be for the better.

So if you're ready to get started, you bring the love, I'll bring the skills and together let's see if we can indeed create a masterpiece.

PART 1

Reclaiming Your Personal Power

First we form habits, then they form us. Conquer your bad habits, or they'll eventually conquer you.

-Dr. Rob Gilbert

Make Love Not War

That old law about an "eye for an eye" leaves everybody blind.

-Martin Luther King, Jr.

PART ONE: RECLAIMING YOUR PERSONAL POWER

You know how unresolved conflict can erode your relationship's well-being? Trapped in a cycle of arguments, debates, rationalizations, and justifications, the goodwill that once existed between you and your partner slowly but surely begins to slip through your fingers. Somehow your adeptness at debate and blame takes on more importance than your ability to love and support.

Procrastination, thoughtlessness, irresponsible behavior, even deception begin to take up more and more space in your relationship. You both agree that therein lies the problem. "If only you would do what we agreed upon..."

"If only you would be nicer to me..." "If only you would be more understanding..." "Why don't you ever think of me?"

And so you both willingly retrace each other's footsteps, none too happy to point out the fallacy in the other's thinking or actions. Implied in of all this is the solution for creating a great relationship that sounds something like this, "If only you would do, act, or think differently, then I would..."

Your partner explains, "It's just my nature." Or "You're making too much of this." Or you may have been told before, "You're being too sensitive."

But it feels so very much more than that to you. It feels mean-spirited, almost punitive. You can't quite put your finger on it, but at times you know there's much more to it than your partner's absent-mindedness. You can't help but think that when you talk about it, there's more left unsaid than said.

The longer the arguments go on, the more the walls go up. Where once there was a foundation of trust and respect, now there's only distance, if not total disconnection. Sadly, it seems that the rare times you do feel connected are the times when the two of you are fighting. Sure, nothing ever gets resolved, but at least for the tiniest of moments there's a spark, a shred of connection.

Your friends shrug their shoulders and say, "You know, relationships are hard work." Hey, hard work is one thing, but this relationship has begun to feel like a chore—a dreaded one at that. Where your relationship was once a port of safe harbor from everything else that life would throw your way, you now are seeking other places of refuge to escape the drudgery of your relationship.

Once full of happiness and hope for a brighter future, you suddenly feel stuck in a quagmire of ill-will and blame. Your hope for a supportive and nourishing relationship has begun to evaporate before your eyes.

And the scary part is you feel powerless to do anything about it. You recognize the patterns because they've happened before. Yet, the patterns seem to have a grip so tight you can't escape their clutch. Spontaneity has been drained from the relationship, replaced by a rote script the two of you willingly stick to.

You know each other's responses by heart. Resignation begins to replace the will to fight. "What's the use, I know what she's going to say," or "Why bother, he'll only get back at me in some other way if I say anything."

It's clear that something has to change. No longer can you easily convince yourself that it's always the other person's fault. Oh sure, you're not ready to let go of the notion that things would be better if your partner would just *get with the program*.

Perhaps an inkling of awareness is beginning to break through—some glint of recognition that you are responsible in part for the conflict that exists in your relationships. And if that's true, then there's an important lesson you need to learn. Afterall, if you've contributed to what the relationship has become, you're just going to keep repeating these patterns wherever you go, with whomever you are with.

The good news is there's a process that you can learn that will enable you to begin to make molehills out of mountains. By mastering this process, you'll discover the joy of reclaiming your personal power in all of your relationships. By using some very simple relationship skills, you'll begin to create long lasting harmony with the people who matter most.

You don't have to say good-bye to your dreams. Relationships no longer have to be sabotaged because you don't know how to break out of a never ending pattern of conflict. There are very simple means available to empower yourself in lessening the amount of discord between you and your partner.

As you master these simple skills I'm about to share with you, you'll immediately notice how much better you'll feel about yourself and your partner. A sense of hopefulness and well-being will replace the gray cloud that hangs over your relationship. You'll rediscover how good it feels to be with your partner. A sense of openness and freedom will begin to replace the self-protective walls that have left you feeling so alone.

Just imagine how good it would feel to see your partner again as a friend, lover, and confidant, rather than the enemy. You need no longer fear *being made wrong* every time you say, think, feel, or do something. Sanity can replace what was once only hurt, anger, betrayal, and rage.

Sound too good to be true? Don't question any of it for even a moment. I'm going to show you some simple steps. These steps can transform many of the booby traps in your relationships. You'll begin to see problems as opportunities to enrich your relationships by developing stronger connections with the people who matter most.

As we go through this journey together, you'll discover an incredible vein of riches. For this is not merely a how-to book that outlines a series of techniques to mechanically apply to the conflicts in your relationships. Rather, this book will illuminate a path of personal empowerment—the means to reclaim your personal power and enrich your emotional and spiritual well-being. This path will be illuminated by the glow cast from your process of self-discovery.

As a result of reading this book, you'll discover more about who you are. This process of self-discovery will shed light on how your unarticulated aches and pains appear in your relationships. As a voice is given to all of those unacknowledged aches and pains, you'll discover what their true source is. And as a result of your self-discovery, you'll develop a better awareness of the choices you have when those aches and pains begin to overwhelm you and, ultimately, the well-being of your relationships.

That's my wish for you, that you have a menu of choices. The knowledge that you no longer have to suffer silently as your relationships become mired in a cloud of never-ending futility. Simply put, this book is a testimony to the power of healing that comes from your willingness to exercise different choices in order to resolve the discord in your relationships.

Little by little you'll begin to see you and your partner's behavior as something more than mere forgetfulness or thoughtlessness. You'll begin to appreciate how often a word slipped in here, an action perpetrated there, are not mere innocent slights.

You'll discover how your actions are embedded in a mosaic. A mosaic that expresses the larger picture of your emotional hurt—the pain that you feel but do not express for whatever good reasons you may have.

Finally, this book is a testimony to the emancipation you can create by mastering the simple relationship skills that will transform how you and your partner work together to build a stronger relationship. Your freedom will emerge from a new found sense of empowerment born from the seeds of self-confidence and self-love. These are the seeds that will give birth to the far more fulfilling tommorows in your life.

No More Skillet Calling the Kettle Black

*Kindness can become its own motive.
We are made kind by being kind.*

-Eric Hoffer

Our relationships are the foundation on which our emotional and spiritual well-being is built. Meaningful, cooperative relationships are the cornerstone of an emotionally healthy life, rich with purpose and love. And you know, these kind of relationships don't just happen, they're created. They're molded and shaped, crafted and nurtured. Strong connections are crafted by two people who believe that the rewards far outweigh the risks of getting close to one another—the risks precipitated by two people forging a bond woven from the strands of emotional honesty, emotional intimacy, and emotional vulnerability.

This bond is woven with the use of special tools—specific relationship skills. These relationship skills enable us to repair, maintain, and nurture the well-being of our relationships. These skills bridge the gap between mistrust and trust, misunderstanding and understanding, self-centeredness and empathy, and hurt and forgiveness.

If you asked Judy what impact the relationship skills she learned in her Relationship Bridge-Builders group had upon her life, she wouldn't explain it the way I would, but she could say it far more eloquently. Judy would simply say, "I learned how to love and be loved."

Far less technical, yet far more poignant than anything I could have come up with. For Judy that was the essence of what had changed for her—the ability to love and be loved. So much of her life had been spent keeping the world at arm's length. Never letting anyone get close enough to care about her. Never opening herself enough to somebody else to care about them. No, Judy had fabricated her own safe place in the world, never believing that it could ever be any different.

But all the hurt and disappointment that came with her involvement with the people in her life had been magically transformed. Transformed from fear and mistrust to self-confidence in her ability to cope with the inevitable difficulties that arise in any relationship. No longer did she feel a prisoner to the ebb and flow of her relationships, a rhythm that so often left her feeling powerless and out of control.

Judy had rediscovered her voice, of equal importance the means to articulate her emotional needs at those times that she was feeling most depleted. For so long, fear controlled her willingness to say out loud what she needed from another person. Too many times she had been laughed at, met with judgment or anger, or worst of all, totally ignored.

Judy had finally said good-bye to the days of her simmering anger. Those were the days when resentment had consumed her as she gave and gave while her emotional needs were left to twist in the wind. The red hot embers of anger were slowly replaced by the brilliance of an emerging inner glow. This glow was given birth by Judy's willingness to boldly put herself out there.

No longer content with being a good sport, she had discovered a place within herself that enabled her to feel entitled. This entitlement fueled her courage to slowly but surely invite people into her world who would honor her voice. A voice that proclaimed her rights as a person. A voice that empowered her to no longer settle for the *status quo* in her relationships.

PART ONE: RECLAIMING YOUR PERSONAL POWER

No, if you asked Judy, she would look you right in the face and tell you flat out, "The *status quo* was forbidden."

But Judy could also tell you that it took more than a new attitude to make a difference in her relationships. You don't just wish something different and then it's so. That's certainly how it begins, but that's not where it ends. Judy discovered what you're about to discover— reclaiming your personal power in your relationships requires a lot of know-how. Your *willingness* to create the kind of relationships you desire is the first step. Step number two is *creating a better awareness* of who you are and how your personal issues appear in your relationships. Step number three is *learning the relationship skills* that can emancipate you from the current patterns of confusion and self-sabotage in which you continually find yourself ensnared.

And so it is that this book is dedicated to the proposition that *you too* can learn how to love and be loved. Your relationships don't have to burn out like a white hot comet that initially glows so brightly, but eventually crashes and burns. Maintaining the passion in your relationships is not a passive process. Anyone, let me repeat, *anyone* can learn how to sustain the well-being of their relationship. You simply need to better understand how your relationship gets stuck. More importantly, you need to learn how to navigate beyond the rocks in the choppy waters on which your relationships run aground.

Getting Beyond Good Intentions

All worthwhile men have good thoughts, good ideas, and good intentions, but precious few of them ever translate those into action.

-John Hancock Field

PART ONE: RECLAIMING YOUR PERSONAL POWER

What are the circumstances in your relationship that bring you to your knees? Those circumstances that never seem to change, in fact many times, trying to change them only makes matters worse. Does the word *powerless* come to mind—a feeling so pervasive it overloads your emotional circuits? Feeling totally ineffectual. Anything you do or say has no impact. Nothing seems to make a dent. The spirit of cooperation that once existed between you and your partner has been replaced by the corrosive cycle of blame/defend, accuse/justify, attack/retaliate, and finally, withdraw/punish.

Is there anyone who hasn't experienced that familiar feeling of frustration over and over again—frustrated that you and your partner just can't seem to get beyond what keeps the two of you bound in knots. You've talked it to death. Ignoring it only makes you feel worse. You've tried to convince yourself that you just won't care about it anymore, but that's like seeing how long you can go without inhaling.

How well does any of that work for you? It's unlikely that any of those strategies are very rewarding in the long run. Why? It's likely that you aren't using the relationship skills that can easily enable you and your partner to stop hurting each other.

It's my most fervent belief that much of the pain that you experience in your relationships can be alleviated if you master a few simple skills. Quite simply, there are specific skills that you can learn that will make relationships less conflictual, if, you're willing to use them.

Let me emphasize that last point. You *must* be *willing* to create relationships with people that are dedicated to *resolving* rather than *perpetuating* conflict. Sadly, not all people are *willing* to surrender the emotional benefits they experience from being in a conflict-filled relationship. But I can tell you this much. Even if you're willing to be in a conflict-free relationship, if you don't know and use the skills necessary to keep a relationship open and growing, you'll find your best intentions undermined.

So the first point I want to make is that you need more than *good intentions* to create relationships that are nourishing. There's a very simple saying I have, "You must work differently at your relationships, not harder at them." If all you do is continue to try and solve the challenges in your relationships the same way you always have, then you will continually get the same results.

For many of you, the skills that I'm going to discuss with you will create different outcomes than those of your old strategies. Learning these skills can change the way you and your partner respond to each other. By changing the way you respond to each other, you can insure a different outcome than you are currently experiencing.

So the first step towards ending the discord in your relationship is *resolving to do things differently.* It's likely that some of your old ways aren't working. But I promise you, there are new skills that can get you over the hump.

Now it's not enough that I believe this. It's not enough that I can see the benefits of mastering these simple skills. You need to be able to see what's in it for you. So let's stop and think about this for a moment. How will you benefit by learning a different way of responding to your partner when the two of you are stuck in familiar patterns of conflict? Can you envision using these familiar patterns as opportunities to *understand* each other rather than to *defeat* each other?

Let's stop here for a moment. Try to focus on exactly what is to be gained by stopping the fighting and bickering. Do more than think about it. Take the time to put it on paper. The reason for this is simple. You'll refer to these pages time and time again when your resolve wavers. Seeing is believing. Being able to reference why you're doing all of this hard work when you feel frustrated, will inspire you to stay on your path. Use the space below to write down how you'll benefit by learning how to resolve your misunderstandings differently with a few new relationship skills.

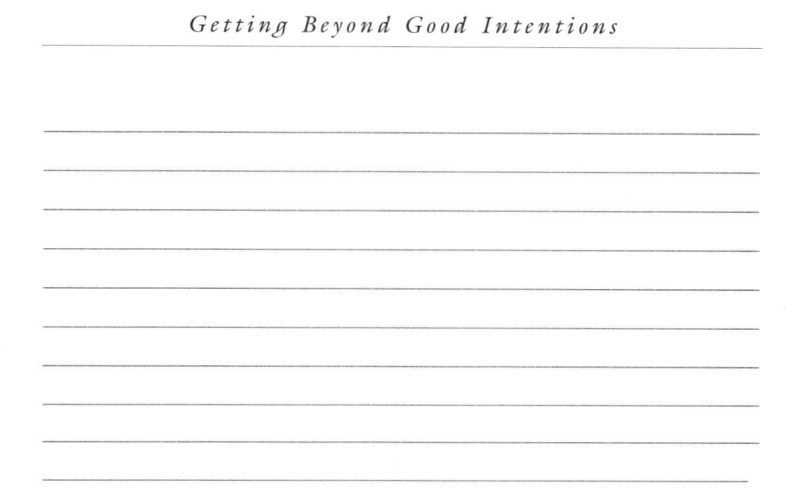

I know how challenging this work is. Maintaining your optimism for change, your hopefulness for well-being, and your belief that you can effectively use these new skills is essential to your success. Whenever you feel your spirit wavering, refer back to these pages. Knowing how you'll benefit by creating different ways of solving problems in your relationship will buoy your spirits when you're feeling paralyzed by discouragement.

I know you possess the necessary courage to weather the dark storms. There are times when you're going to feel awkward. From time-to-time your partner may not be as supportive as you would like them to be. Moving out of the familiar and into the unknown is enough to make anybody take pause.

Fear has the same effect on us all. We stop dead in our tracks. Looking for a way to retreat, self-protection becomes our number one goal. And eventually we'll reach for ol' faithful—our old habits. Not because those old habits are effective, simply because they're familiar.

I'm proposing a new standard. From here on out, commit to using skills that are effective rather than merely familiar. Don't settle for the comfort of what you know best, venture into the realm of the new and unknown. I realize what I'm asking of you. But if you can just hang on to your belief in the benefits that you listed above, you'll feel less unsure of yourself and more encouraged to venture forward.

As you embrace the formula I've just suggested, you'll begin to notice subtle changes. Your fear will lessen. Your confidence will increase. Those old ways will be less seductive as you discover you have more and more choices. Ultimately, you'll discover that the more choices you have to resolve the conflicts in your relationship, the more empowered you'll feel. And believe me, there isn't a better gift in the world that you can give yourself.

PART 2

Pinpointing the Issue

*Since nothing we intend is ever faultless,
and nothing we attempt ever without
error, and nothing we achieve
without some measure of finitude and
fallibility we call humanness,
we are saved by forgiveness.*

-David Augsburger

The Most Important Choice of All

Anybody can become angry—that is easy; but to be angry with the right person, and to the right degree, and at the right time, and for the right purpose, and in the right way—that is not within everybody's power and is not easy.

-Aristotle

PART TWO: PINPOINTING THE ISSUE

Let me caution you as you begin to read the three chapters in this section. They each deserve your undivided attention. Take your time with the information I present to you. Use your highlighter. Write notes in the margins. Do the exercises. But most importantly, take your time. Be patient. Be kind to yourself. Self-forgiveness will be your greatest ally in our new adventure. There's an unfortunate truism about learning, you'll inevitably struggle in the beginning. You and I both expect it to be that way, so there will be no surprises. Every mistake you make along the way will not be an indictment of you or these new skills, only a necessary step to your final destination.

There's good reason to mix caution with your enthusiasm. The skills that I'm going to discuss with you throughout this book are so potent, they're so empowering, your mastery of them will change the tone of your relationships forever. Please, please, don't set yourself up to fail by creating initial expectations that are too high for both you and your partner. This is a time for both of you to be kind to and encouraging of each other.

Okay, with that said, I'm going to talk about a very specific relationship skill that's the bridge between unresolved and resolved conflict. It's the core relationship skill used in the process of making molehills out of mountains. I call it *pinpointing the issue*. Let that sink in for a moment. Don't go rushing into the rest of the material. Try and focus on those three words, *pinpoint-*

ing the issue. In time, this phrase is going to be one of your greatest allies, an ally that will empower you, enabling you to create relationships that are less conflictual, more fulfilling.

Now take your time with the following point I'm about to make. This point is *the* fundamental premise of pinpointing the issue. In order to resolve many of the unresolved issues in your relationships, you must understand what I'm going to tell you next. *Most of the conflict that exists between two people has two levels to it, not just one.*

The first level is the precipitating event of the conflict, which I refer to as the *circumstance.* The second level is the oftentimes unacknowledged aspect of the conflict, which I refer to as the underlying relationship issue. The *underlying relationship issue* is an issue that lies hidden beneath the surface of the event or circumstance that precipitates an argument. The relationship between the circumstance that precipitates the conflict and the underlying relationship issue is like the saying about a wolf dressed in sheep's clothing. The underlying relationship issue is the wolf, it's simply dressed in sheep's clothing—the circumstance, so that it may better hide its presence.

Pinpointing the issue is the relationship skill you will use to resolve conflict by identifying the *two levels* that exist in most of your conflicts. As you're better able to identify these two levels, you'll find that you have a choice about which level to focus on when you try to problem-solve with your partner.

Why, you might be wondering, should you care

PART TWO: PINPOINTING THE ISSUE

whether there are different levels to the conflict you experience with your partner? Afterall, you might be thinking to yourself, all I'm interested in is being able to watch the TV shows I want to watch, or what's the big deal if I leave the toilet seat up or down, or what does it matter if you squeeze the tube of toothpaste from the middle or the end of the tube.

Here's what's in it for you. Focusing your problem-solving efforts on *both* levels will enable you to more effectively resolve your relationship issues with your partner. This premise is critical to the process of making molehills out of mountains. Until now, it may be that you have only considered the fact that there's only one level while totally ignoring the second level. The very reason so much remains unresolved between you and your partner is because *both* levels of the conflict don't get addressed. Until you address *both* levels of the conflict, it's likely that you'll remain stuck with your partner in a vicious cycle, unable to resolve the core of the problems that are present in your relationship.

Being able to identify, as well as talk about, both levels will lessen the building tensions between you and your partner. It's easy to see why that would be. Inevitably, there are important unresolved relationship issues that lurk beneath the surface of those seemingly petty examples I mentioned above. Relationship issues that are smoldering and festering, patiently waiting for you and your partner to acknowledge their very existence, taking up more and more space in your relationship, the longer you choose to ignore their presence.

Unfortunately, most of us spend all of our time spinning in circles, focusing only on the surface level of the discord.

What you need to understand is that most conflicts that remain unresolved between you and your partner do so because you're focusing solely on the surface level without addressing the issues that lurk beneath the surface.

What I want you to understand at this point in time is the following: *when you and your partner are stuck, when you are repeatedly visiting unresolved issues, it's likely that the issues that you're talking about are not the issues that you need to be talking about.* Quite simply, you need to shift the focus from the circumstances of your conflict to the underlying relationship issues that are hidden in the events that precipitate the conflict.

Let me give you a short, simple example to try and make a complex idea a little more understandable for you. A man continually promises his wife that he'll take their dirty laundry to the dry cleaners. Yet time after time, he *forgets* to take it, leaving it for his totally exasperated wife to take care of. Each time he forgets, she becomes angry with her husband. Time after time they try to create a plan to ensure that the husband will follow through on his promise, time after time he doesn't follow through.

This maddening circle continues. The reason why it never gets resolved is because the husband and wife focus only on *one* level of the conflict, the *circumstance,* which is the problem of how he can get the dry cleaning to the cleaners. However, they completely ignore the second level of the argument which is the *underlying relationship issue.*

Let's take a look at what the *second level* to the conflict might be. If you asked the husband to talk about how he feels about his wife and the relationship, he might say that

PART TWO: PINPOINTING THE ISSUE

he feels like his wife is always on his back. He believes that she never *appreciates* the things that he *does* do for her. In fact, he believes she only focuses on the things that he *doesn't* do.

If you asked the wife what she feels about her husband and the relationship she may tell you that she feels like she is being *taken for granted*. She feels more like an errand boy for her husband rather than his lover. Both husband and wife are feeling unappreciated by each other, but they never take the time to talk to each other about their hurt. They only focus on the dry cleaning, which is the *circumstance*, not the *underlying relationship issue*, which is feeling unappreciated by one another.

What's the big deal, you may be wondering. Let me ask you this, is the dry cleaning the sole issue worthy of this couple's focus or are the relationship issues that I just mentioned likely to be *as important*? Furthermore, if you agree that the most important focus of discussion needs to be on the relationship issues, how likely is it that the dry cleaning problem will go away until they begin to focus on them?

To bring this discussion full circle, experience has taught me the way out of this trap is by mastering the relationship skill: *pinpointing the issue*. This skill will enable you to step out of the cycle of futile arguments, unkept promises, and angry reactions. And the secret to pinpointing the issue, the first necessary step is accepting the fact that there are two levels to most conflicts: the circumstance and the inevitable underlying relationship issues.

Let's take a moment and practice identifying the two levels of conflict by looking at the following scenarios.

Scenario #1

A husband tries to limit the dollar amount his wife spends on her credit card. She shows her husband who the boss is by digging her heels in and refusing to change her spending habits.

The circumstance: Disagreeing over how much money the wife can spend.
The underlying relationship issue: Power and control about who is going to tell who how much money they can or cannot spend.

Scenario #2

A parent criticizes a child for getting one *C* while ignoring the five *A*s the child received on their report card. The child responds by getting all *D*s on their next report card.

The circumstance: The parent harps on the one *C* the child gets on their report card and does not acknowledge the good work the child did in other areas.

The underlying relationship issue: The child feels unappreciated for his overall effort so the child *gets even* by not trying at all.

Scenario #3

A man belittles a woman for her beliefs about abortion.

The circumstance: Two people have an honest disagreement about their views on abortion.
The underlying relationship issue: The man's intolerance leaves the woman feeling judged and unaccepted.

Scenario #4

A man continually threatens to end his relationship with his partner every time an argument occurs between the two of them. His partner begins to resent this man for refusing to have more of a commitment to the relationship. The partner's resentment repeatedly spills over onto the man, perpetuating the arguing and inevitable threats.

The circumstance: The man's reaction to conflict with his partner.

The underlying relationship issue: The partner's unmet emotional need of being able to feel safe without the threat of the man leaving the relationship anytime an argument breaks out.

Focusing on *both* levels of a conflict is a new way to think about more effectively resolving conflict. Think what that would mean to you. Think for a moment what any of your relationships would be like if you had more time and energy to put into nurturing them rather than furiously trying to plug every leak that springs.

Let your imagination run wild for a moment. What would your life look like if you felt more in control of yourself and the way you resolved issues with the people in your life? In my mind, there's only one thing that gets in your way—not effectively applying the relationship skills that will resolve the inevitable conflicts that arise in your life.

Are you beginning to see why it's so important to be able to distinguish between the two levels that exist in most conflict? As I said before, these relationship issues live beneath the surface of the events in your relationship. They oftentimes go untalked about between you and your partner. Because these issues lay beneath the surface, oftentimes unknown to you and your partner, you'll necessarily create a way for the pain caused by those underlying issues to be expressed. The way that they get expressed is a special code. That code inevitably is the misunderstandings and petty arguments that appear and reappear in your relationships.

PART TWO: PINPOINTING THE ISSUE

For now, think of the underlying relationship issues as the emotional *owwies* of your relationship. Sometimes you know that you're hurting, sometimes not. Sometimes you're aware of what you're hurting about, sometimes not. Whatever is true for you, that pain doesn't sit idly by waiting to be noticed.

Pain is energy. Energy that needs to be discharged. Our goal is to discharge it by learning how to talk about it with our partner rather than acting it out against our partner.

I have a saying, "Those feelings that we don't verbalize, we'll act out." If you choose not to verbalize the pain you're feeling from the underlying relationship issue, you'll inevitably choose to express it in behaviors that tend to spark even more discord between you and your partner. It's those circumstances that perpetuate much of the unresolved problems that undermine the well-being of your relationships.

The way out of the cycle of self-sabotage is the skill I mentioned above, pinpointing the issue by addressing *both* levels of the conflict. This relationship skill is so important that I want to recap the process involved with this skill: 1) recognize that there are *two* levels to most relationship discord; 2) distinguish between the two levels which are the specific *circumstance* that precipitated the discord with your partner and the *underlying relationship issue* that is embedded in the event or circumstance; 3) recognize that you have a choice whether to stay stuck in trying to *fix* the never ending *circumstance* or *resolve* the unexpressed *underlying relationship issue*.

That's the process of pinpointing the issue. The next two chapters of this section will focus more specifically on the circumstance and the underlying relationship issues. In section seven I will walk you through exactly how to pinpoint the issue. I will also suggest some tools to use once you've made the choice to focus on the relationship issue *as well as* the circumstance. But for now let's conclude with a bit of wisdom my good friend Max once told me, "Steve, you can't do the *boot scoot boogie* with your dance partner until you understand what the fiddler is a fiddlin'."

Separating the Wheat from the Chaff

The latter part of a wise man's life is taken up in curing the follies, prejudices, and false opinions he had contracted in the former.

-Jonathan Swift

PART TWO: PINPOINTING THE ISSUE

Okay. Here's what we've established so far. Making molehills out of mountains is facilitated by a relationship skill called pinpointing the issue. Hopefully, you're beginning to consider that there are two levels to most conflicts between you and your partner. The two levels? The circumstances at the surface of the conflict and the underlying relationship issues beneath the surface. The goal of pinpointing the issue? Making a distinction between these two levels as you try to resolve your conflicts. The reason to do so? To create an important choice for you and your partner to make. The choice? To focus your conflict resolution efforts solely on *fixing* the circumstances of the discord or to focus an equal amount of attention on *resolving* the underlying relationship issue embedded in the event that precipitated the discord.

If it seems to you that I'm repeating myself, you're right, but for a very good reason. I can't impress upon you how powerful this skill can be for you. I want to make sure that you have an opportunity to give it your most careful consideration. What we're trying to do is develop a new habit. The elements of creating that good habit are repetition and time. The payoff for you is less hurt and confusion as you master the formula for untangling the knots that eventually entangle two people.

Okay? So let's continue by zeroing in on the surface level of any discord—the *circumstance* that precipitates the discord. For example, it could be you repeatedly promise to do some household chores, but you never get around to doing them. Or your partner continually keeps you waiting, no matter how many times you've told them how angry it makes you feel when they're late. Perhaps you're never able to reach agreement about some aspect of how you raise your children.

In these three examples, there's a circumstance that precipitates some level of discord between you and your partner. In the first example, the circumstance is not doing your chores. In the second example, the circumstance is continually standing your partner up. And in the third example, the circumstance is never agreeing on whether your child should play soccer or learn to play the piano. Very simply, disagreements start with some circumstance that arises from the day-to-day life events between you and your partner.

The thing about the event that triggers any conflict is that it often serves as a smoke screen for all that goes untalked about, yet desperately needs to be focused on, between you and your partner. You certainly know how cloudy and confusing things can get in the heat of the moment. But all that really does is sustain the stalemate. Let's see if the following conflict between Laurie and Jamie makes my point. You can be sure that some variation of this dialogue goes on in millions of homes.

"Jamie, you promised you were going to stop drinking," Laurie said.

"I didn't say I would stop. I said I would drink only under certain conditions. That's what you and I agreed to. At least that's the way I remember it," Jamie said, his voice shaking as he spoke.

"You may be right, but you haven't honored any part of what we agreed to. Not only have you not honored our agreement, I feel like you're throwing it in my face. I feel like you're belittling me," Laurie shouted back.

"Listen, forget all that noise. You haven't given me one reason to be nice to you. You're constantly on my back. You go through my pockets counting my money. You smell my breath when I come home from work every night. You don't think I know about how you've been calling my friends, checking up on me?

"You're the one to blame here. You aren't giving me the space I need to find my way out of this. How dare you treat me the way you've been treating me! What right do you have to check up on me the way you have been? That's what has to stop around here. The problem isn't when and how much I drink, the problem is you and your unwillingness to give me any space.

"I can quit drinking anytime I want to. You just aren't willing to give me the credit. You're always riding my back. That's what has to stop around here."

"Jamie, whoa, slow down just one second here. I refuse to keep caving in to your bullying tactics. The issue *is* your drinking, it's not my behavior. I have to sneak around because you won't be honest with me."

By now Jamie's eyes were bulging as he said, "So you admit it. You admit that you've been sneaking around, checking up on me."

"Of course I do, but so what. All of this is beside the point," she responded defensively.

"No, it's precisely the point. I'm going to keep drinking until I decide it's time to stop. There are no other points to be made. And you *will* stop checking up on me or else...." his voice trailed off, waving a menacing finger in the air.

That's usually where I enter the picture with a couple. Trying to help undo the stalemate. The mechanism used to sustain the stalemate, you ask? Quite simply, focusing only on fixing the circumstance without attempting to resolve the underlying relationship issue. And believe me, the stalemate doesn't happen by accident. Most importantly, we have to learn what *our investment* is in maintaining the stalemate.

Did I just say, learn what *our investment* in the stalemate is? Absolutely. Now I'm suggesting something very big here. Do not dismiss it without carefully considering how it might be true.

I'm suggesting it's time to think about things differently than perhaps you have in the past. Think this through with me. Why do you spend so much time and energy trying *only* to fix the circumstance, the precipitant of the conflict? Why do you so willingly continue to invest yourself in a process of resolution that brings you everything *but* resolution? Why do you keep spinning in circles, chasing after some magical solution that doesn't exist?

Here's how I look at things. There's nothing that we do, think, or feel that doesn't bring us some kind of emotional benefit. It's critical that you open yourself up to this point. Everything we do provides us some sort of payoff. Therefore, focusing *only* on the circumstance, doing everything you can to fix a person, a problem, or both, while ignoring the underlying relationship issue, has some kind of emotional benefit, some kind of emotional payoff.

I'm sure you must be thinking that I'm off my rocker. Why, oh why, Steve, would I willingly involve myself in so much pain and frustration, you ask? Yes, I know how frustrating it is to be caught in a vicious cycle of unresolved conflict, but perhaps it's time to consider whether or not you've eagerly agreed to do the dance.

So, don't dismiss my assertion just yet. Think for a moment, what's so attractive about remaining stuck in the quagmire? Here's one thought for you to chew on: the quagmire certainly can become familiar territory. You probably have your part down pat. You may even know the script by heart. And it leaves much about what needs to be talked about by you and your partner safely tucked away, the bomb remains ticking, but left undetonated for another day. For example...

Stanley and I had met at our favorite watering hole a couple of Sundays ago. We hadn't seen each other in a few months, so he was bringing me up to date on his life. We liked getting together to grouse about our frustrations, play some darts, take in a game on the big screen. While waiting for the Cubs to come on, I asked him how things were going with his wife.

"S.O.S., kiddo. Same ol', same ol', man, nothing changes with us," Stanley said, a look of indifference punctuating his response.

"I can't tell if that's good or bad," I replied.

"Ech, who knows any more. There's something heavy hanging in the air between the two of us. Ever since I shot her down a while back, telling her I didn't what to start a family right now. I told you how she got on that kick of hers again, wanting to have children. She's been, I don't know, remote, someway, somehow, I'm not sure how. She's there but not really there. I can't quite put my finger on it, but it's there, you know what I mean?"

Stanley asked, seemingly searching for his own understanding more than trying to explain the situation to me.

"There's this tension between us. I guess more importantly there isn't any lightness anymore. Sometimes there's nothing at all.

"Take tonight for example, I'll go home, she'll half-heartedly yell at me for being out with you. You know how she hates me being with you. She thinks that we're sitting around, ganging up on her. Then I'll tell her how sorry I am. Then she'll tell me that I better never do it again. Then I'll tell her she's right, it won't happen again. Then she'll give me her look of disgust. Then I'll go off and watch TV. She'll shake her head and ignore me until Thursday. I'll stay out of her way, not wanting to turn this into anything heavy. By Saturday, she'll find some other way I've disappointed her and then start the dance all over again."

One, two, cha, cha, cha. Three, four, cha, cha, cha. They've got the dance down pat. Frozen in time, their relationship is sitting on a powder keg, yet neither of them wants to go near it. They settle for indifference, polite apathy, subtle tension, and ever-increasing distance. The reason why? My friend, I suggest to you one reason and one reason only. Fear!

Isn't that what really needs to be overcome? Our fear of what isn't stated? We're so fearful of having to put on the table things that may make us uncomfortable. So we devise ways of dancing around the underlying relationship issue, over it, under it, through it, behind it. We're afraid our emotions will get out of control, we're afraid we'll be ridiculed or, even worse, ignored. Ultimately, we're afraid of the unknown becoming known.

That's why we stay so focused on merely attempting to fix the problem. It's a known quantity. We know the path backwards and forwards. We come up with ingenious ways to rectify problematic behavior. There's a certain seduction in focusing exclusively on the circumstance of an argument.

Although there are many reasons for that, let me advance one more premise that I believe locks two people in a death grip over the circumstances of their disagreements at the expense of focusing on the underlying relationship issue. The ever tantalizing myth—control. Focusing only on fixing the problem is a way to do the dance—the dance of attempting to control someone's behavior, words, feelings, or thoughts. And therein lies the problem. There's no solution that I know of to an underlying relationship issue that includes your ability to *control* your partner's behavior.

That's why trying to fix the circumstance without resolving the underlying issue is so ineffective. The only solution to fixing the circumstance is *dealing with the underlying issue*. But let me ask you, what seems like a more familiar way to problemsolve for you, attempting to control who your partner is, does, says, thinks, and feels or peeling back the scabs of the underlying relationship issue?

Can you see the mirage that the myth of control creates? It's total misdirection. Take some time to think about this. Let your mind wander with my next question. Think about all the time, all the emotional energy, think about all of *you* that you've invested in the following simple proposition. It sounds something like this, "If I fix the problem, if I fix the person, if I can come up with just the right way of saying what I have to say, then I won't have to feel this continual pain that the circumstances of my relationship creates for me."

Have you ever taken notice just how ineffective this is? Have you ever noticed that any strategy aimed at fixing the problem without resolving the underlying relationship issues is like squeezing a balloon full of water. All you do is slosh the problem around from one side to the other, but the problem never goes away. Push the problem down there, it pops up again over here. Threaten it away, plead for it to go away, or cajole it away, it makes me no-never-mind, because it will transform itself into a more virulent reincarnation.

The reason by now should be plain. Any attempts at controlling the person or the situation is not dealing with the root of the problem—the underlying relationship issue.

If you read my book *Building Better Bridges*, you know that I devoted a whole chapter to personal freedom and the destructive influence that control exerts on the emotional climate of our relationships. I have a Bridge-Builder's Tip in the chapter that reads, *If you place demands on a person to change, can you see how you will require that person to lie to you?* Please heed this tip as you find yourself trapped in trying to fix the circumstance of an argument rather than resolve the underlying relationship issue.

I want to advance one more reason the circumstance of an argument is a much safer place to focus on rather than the underlying relationship issue. It freezes the relationship in time. Nothing changes. Everything stays the same.

Now I can hear you shouting at me. I can hear your protests. Why would I want this mess to stay the same?

PART TWO: PINPOINTING THE ISSUE

Why would I be reading this book and every other book I have read? Why would anyone want to live in the hell that I've been living in? Well, I can only respond by saying, "Me thinketh thou doth protest too much!"

Here's a short answer. Fear. Fear of what moving forward with your partner may mean. Fear of what the next level of your relationship may look like. Even a bigger fear for many of you, fear that if you worked through the relationship issues that live and breathe beneath the surface, your relationship would be over.

Now stop at this point. Does anything I've said in the last paragraph ring true for you? Think your way through this. I'm offering you an important window to look through. There's much freedom on the other side of that window if you can only glean what your investment is in keeping the relationship stuck on the surface level.

What are the circumstances that appear and reappear in your relationship—circumstances that merely serve to freeze your relationship in time? Take a moment and write down what conflicts appear and reappear in your relationship.

_____
_____
_____
_____
_____
_____
_____
_____
_____
_____

Now, think for a moment. What purpose does focusing solely on the circumstances of the conflict in your relationship serve you? Does it help you or your partner to remain in control, does it freeze your relationship in time, and/or does it give you a role to play in your relationship? Perhaps there's some other angle you may be working? All I know is how helpful it is to take ownership of what you're getting out of the dance.

You can see how important that is, can't you? The work we do throughout this book is geared towards one thing and one thing only—helping you create new choices that will enable you to get your needs met, as well as having an alternative to sabotaging your relationship.

Go ahead and put it on paper. Write about the investment you have in continually revisiting the circumstances of your relationship discord without focusing on the underlying relationship issues.

_____
_____
_____
_____
_____
_____
_____
_____
_____
_____
_____
_____

I hope I am keeping things simple here for purposes of my explaining these important concepts to you. But in doing so, I don't mean to minimize the complexity of the problems that you're dealing with in your life. I understand how confusing it can get for you when things that are so black and white in this book aren't so black and white in your life.

But please be assured that if you take your time with this information, you'll discover what I've discovered over the last ten years. You'll discover what we're building together is not a mere understanding of a self-help technique, but a blueprint for your path to reclaiming your personal power and a means by which you can return a sense of stability to your life.

Where There's Smoke There's Fire

If the core of conflict between two people is denied or suppressed, the relationship itself will become sick, whether it be subtle or obvious, sooner or later, the relationship will always suffer when the core of the conflict goes unacknowledged.

-Stanley Phillips

I hope it's becoming clear that there's a different way to think about the conflict that exists between you and your partner. And as that shift begins to take place within, can you see the possibilities that come with this new way of thinking about the dance that you and your partner do with each other?

Therein lies the key—being open to what's possible for you by simply readjusting your focus from the surface event to the underlying relationship issue. Let me remind you that the skills discussed throughout this book are the means by which you can transform your relationships. However, the most important derivative of mastering these skills, first and foremost, is developing a better understanding of yourself.

Now I hear those gears churning. Why, pray tell, is it so important for me to have a better understanding of myself, you may be thinking? Afterall, so much of the conflict between me and my partner would be alleviated if my partner would simply act differently. However, if you accept that much of the conflict that exists in your relationship is about the underlying relationship issues rather than the mere circumstance, then it's important that you begin to understand yourself better.

Self-knowledge is the prescription I write for anybody who's seeking to create significant shifts in their relationships. Do you clearly understand what your fears about emotional intimacy are? Do you understand how your emotional discomfort shows up in your relationship? Is that discomfort even acknowledged by you? Does it get expressed? If it gets expressed, is it verbalized or acted out? Can you see the path I'm suggesting in order to effectively make molehills out of mountains?

Let me first tell you what the path is not. The process of making molehills out of mountains is not making your partner out to be wrong. Blaming and shaming merely fuels the fire rather than puts it out. Are you ready to surrender your unwillingness to take responsibility for your words and deeds? That's a prerequisite for all of this work. If you truly want to learn how to resolve your differences, you no longer get to go through life being an *expert* on everybody but yourself.

Do you get what I mean by being an expert on everybody but yourself? Is there anybody reading this book that doesn't spend an inordinate amount of time *explaining* their partner to their partner? What a wonderful way to pass the time. The only question I have is, are you getting any closer to understanding yourself as you spend most of your time in your partner's head? I have never, ever, not once seen anything good come from one person getting into another person's head. But let me tell you what I have seen work time after time.

Focusing on yourself. Knowing yourself. Knowing how your issues, your *craziness*, gets provoked and ultimately activated in your relationships. Do you know what fears you have about connecting with another human being? Do you know what essential truths about who you are are at the core of the chaos that you create? Do you know enough about who you are to express that to your partner rather than act it out?

You see, we're back to that choice thing again. Making molehills out of mountains is a series of choices.

Choosing to know yourself. Choosing to stay out of your partner's head. Choosing to talk about your fears rather than acting them out. Choosing to focus on the underlying relationship issues rather than the events that precipitate the conflict. I hope I've made a compelling enough case that self-knowledge is the foundation upon which resolving conflict is based. So with that as a premise, let's explore what the underlying relationship issues are and how they uniquely present themselves in your life.

First, here are four themes for the underlying relationship issues you can count on living and breathing beneath the surface of much of the conflict that exists between you and your partner. Those themes are: 1) acceptance; 2) unmet emotional needs; 3) appreciation; 4) power and control. I will speak in more detail about each of these themes in the upcoming sections. For now, let's discuss more broadly what an underlying relationship issue is and why it dwells silently beneath the surface of your relationships.

It's easy to understand why you would prefer to leave the underlying relationship issue hidden, isn't it? Typically, the underlying relationship issue is much more volatile than the circumstance that's being discussed. For example, what would be a safer discussion, why your partner picks a lousy restaurant to go to every Saturday night or why your partner hasn't shown any interest in sex with you in the last twelve months?

Consider this conversation I had with my friend, Max. There's a special beach in the park where everyone goes to exercise their dogs called the *doggie beach*. We take Max's dog, a beautiful blond spaniel, Kaybee, to let her swim in the lake and play with the other dogs. One day as

Kaybee was thrashing around in the water, chasing down an old tennis ball we'd thrown into the lake, Max and I got to talking.

"I really did it this time," Max said in a dejected tone.

"What did you do this time?" I asked Max.

"I stuck my foot in my mouth. I don't think that Teddy will ever forgive me for this one," Max admitted.

"What did you say?" I asked.

Max's voice was coated with remorse. "What did I say, what didn't I say? In fact, that's the whole problem. I said everything but what I wanted to say. But boy, oh boy, what I did say, hoooo, she's never going to let me live this one down."

"Max, I hope you won't be offended if I tell you, I don't know what the hell you're talking about," I said.

As Max began to explain, Kaybee decided to dry herself off on us, shaking her body furiously. Max continued the tale of woe as we toweled down.

"Teddy set up an interview for a job in Seattle. When I found out about that, I flipped out. I felt like things were going so well between us. Then I find out about the interview, well I really felt angry, even hurt. It made me feel so unimportant that she would even consider going so far away."

Pleadingly I asked, "Max, of course you told her about how hurt you were? Max, tell me that you told Teddy how unimportant it made you feel that she would even think about moving away. Max look me in the eyes and tell me you told Teddy that you cared, that you didn't want to risk having such a huge separation."

"Wellllll, not exactly," Max said.

PART TWO: PINPOINTING THE ISSUE

"Well, what exactly did you say?" I asked insistently.

"Steve, in my defense I *thought* all those things that you just said, I just didn't *say* any of those things to Teddy."

"Close only counts in horseshoes and hand grenades," I said with as much support as I could muster.

"Well, I sure detonated one hell of a hand grenade," Max meekly replied.

"Max, please, I'm begging you, please tell me you didn't do what you usually do."

"Well, pretty much so, yea," Max slyly admitted.

"That would be your seemingly innocuous statements that leave everyone guessing at what you're upset about, but no one understanding what it is you're upset about?" I growled at him.

"Oh, that would be," Max responded, equally exasperated.

"Max, just what is it that you told Teddy?"

"I simply said that if you moved to Seattle, then we would have to change the way we communicate. I may have mentioned something about perhaps using smoke signals, pony express, postcards, or perhaps the space shuttle."

"And?"

"I don't remember all that she said, I just remember more of how it was said to me. That's what always seems to stay with me the longest."

By now I was practically scolding Max. "Max, how many times do I have to tell you about this little habit of yours. You can't keep going through life being cute when you have something important to talk over with somebody."

"I know, Steve, believe me I know. But I just can't come out and say what I'm feeling. Afterall, what right do I have to feel so strongly about Teddy. She has repeatedly told me not to expect a thing from our relationship. Besides, I couldn't possibly tell her how important our relationship is to me, afterall, if she doesn't feel the same way, then where am I?"

"I don't know, Max, but it doesn't seem that you could be any worse off than you are now."

"Ohhhhh, I never thought of it that way before."

You know the weird thing was, Max's dog, Kaybee, looked me right in the eye, winked, and shook her head up and down as if in complete agreement with what I just said.

Yes, who isn't an expert at making things worse than they already are? Who hasn't stuck their foot in their mouth because they didn't want to *go there*? And just where is *go there*? It's the dreaded *V* word. Vulnerable.

Who of us doesn't twist ourselves in knots to avoid feeling vulnerable with another human being? Who hasn't turned a relationship inside out, upside down, wreaking havoc, stirring things up with only one end in mind. Avoid feeling vulnerable. Avoid appearing vulnerable. Maintain a position of strength at all times.

That's the kicker, isn't it? Not wanting to appear weak. Not wanting to give an edge to your partner. Do you equate being vulnerable with being weak, setting yourself up to be hurt or taken advantage of?

What are the things that make you feel most vulnerable with your partner? What are the essential truths that you feel, yet are too frightened to reveal? And the basis of the fear is that you don't want to feel so exposed, you don't want to feel so at risk, you don't want to feel so out there.

It's important to take ownership of what those things are. You see, oftentimes, we put so much energy into protecting ourselves, we drain a lot of energy from the relationship itself. Can you can understand how important it is to learn how to balance your need for self-protection with your relationship's need to be free of the energy invested in protecting yourself? More importantly, I hope you can see how avoiding expressing what needs to be expressed has its own way of creating problems between you and your partner.

Let's look at another reason you may choose to leave the underlying relationship issue hidden beneath the surface of the circumstance. It's a means by which the relationship doesn't have to grow, become more intimate, and frankly, many times, more scary. If you never discuss the underlying relationship issues, the relationship will stay stuck right where it is, focused on the reoccurring circumstances. Unfulfilling? Likely, but perhaps the familiar is safer than traveling into the unknown.

Consider this example for a moment. You or your partner are abusing drugs and alcohol. Much of your time and energy is invested in cleaning up after the fallout that inevitably accompanies alcohol and drug abuse. However, it might be safer to deal with the chaos created by substance abuse rather than focus only on the growth and development of your relationship and the resultant tensions that accompanies such growth.

I'm reminded of two old friends of mine who in the end couldn't hold things together. I always believed that fear kept interfering with their ability to sustain their relationship. More importantly, I think their relationship was held hostage to their fears. Ultimately, they went their separate ways, never able to get beyond arguing about how much time Sandy spent at work. This is pretty much how things ended for the two of them.

"I don't understand why you won't admit it," Elly said.

"Admit what?" Sandy asked.

"The truth. The truth about why you spend so much time at work. We go over and over it, and none of it rings true."

"What's not true? My job is demanding. I want to hold up my end of things with you," Sandy patiently explained.

Elly's voice had an edge to it, a weird mixture of hurt, frustration, and hate all rolled into one as she said, "I don't believe a word of it. It feels like you're avoiding me, putting me off. Lately, it feels like you don't even want to be around me."

Sandy had become equally defensive. Both of them had been down this road many times. But today, he was feeling especially boxed in, feeling as if there was nowhere to go with her. "When you keep harping on me the way you do, it sure doesn't make it appealing to come home."

"Don't make this about me. This is about us. This is about your half-baked excuses. This is about whether you're in this relationship or out," Elly pointedly said.

That set Sandy off. That arrow had pierced the heart of the matter, yet he reacted the only way he knew how in order to prevent the truth from coming out—with a great deal of hostility. "In or out! What's there about what I do that would make you even say such a thing?

PART TWO: PINPOINTING THE ISSUE

You need to spend more time getting your head examined and less time focusing on me! In or out—you've really lost it now!"

Elly had dug in this time, determined to get an answer once and for all. There was no turning back, this lack of involvement had to be resolved once and for all. Unwilling to endure this suspended animation any longer, Elly wanted, needed, was demanding a decision. She deserved more and if it wasn't going to be with Sandy, well, so be it. But the dance was going to stop.

By now Elly was screaming, "No, not this time. You're not going to do it to me again. You're not going to flip the tables on me. I don't have to prove anything to you. I'm tired of avoiding this, all the ways we avoid it. I'm asking you point blank. Are you in or out?

"I'm not doing this alone by myself anymore. No more presents to smooth things over, no more half-hearted attempts to be around more. No more drama to get you to say that you love me. Are you in or not? Are you out of here, if so when? We don't need to keep wasting each other's lives on this half-assed attempt at a relationship. All I want is the truth."

Sandy was taken aback by Elly's new found determination. It was slowly sinking in just how serious she was. So he considered very carefully what to say next. There was so much at stake, but the fight had drained from his body. All that was left was a look of resignation.

"Alright, if you put it that way, I guess I should say, I don't want to do this anymore," Sandy mumbled.

"Do what?" Elly said fearfully.

"This, us, you and me. I just don't feel safe doing it with you anymore. It doesn't feel right. I guess that's what I've avoided saying for so long. No, you've been right all along. I'm just too afraid. I don't know how to explain it any better. I don't know what it would look like if I put both feet into the relationship. I don't know how to do it any better than I'm already doing it.

"This is the best I've got, or it's all that I've got, or I don't know, I just don't know. In fairness to you, you're right, I do hide. I hide at work. I hide here at home. There are days when dread just overwhelms me. About what, well you seem to be the expert. But the thought of doing this any differently is just unbearable."

And so it goes. Slowly but surely as the excuses are stripped away, as the circumstances that a person hides behind are lifted, inevitably what crawls out from underneath the surface is some fear, discomfort, or smoldering resentment about the relationship itself. Left undetected, these corrosive elements slowly but surely eat away at the well-being of your relationships. Without focusing on the relationship issues, it must feel like you're doing battle with one arm tied behind your back.

Let's look at one more reason why you may choose to stay paralyzed by the circumstances of your conflicts rather than resolving the underlying relationship issues. Plain ol' being afraid of the consequences of getting honest. Perhaps you fear that if you get honest with your partner, they may emotionally or physically abandon you. Have you ever tried to resolve an issue with somebody and the thanks you got for your efforts was the silent treatment or they just disappeared from your life altogether? How anxious would you be to explore the underlying issues that exist in any other relationships?

How about if we get practical for a moment. Let's take

a break from the theory by practicing for a moment. Take your time with this. You may even need to get some perspective from a friend or family member, but please whoever it is, make sure that they are safe and have only your best interests at heart.

Can you think of a time where you have found yourself in the same disagreement over and over again with your partner? It could be about how you decide where to go on your vacation. It could be how much time you spend on your computer rather than with your partner. It could be how you decide who's going to clean the house. No matter the topic, nothing ever seems to resolve the problem. When you get to this place with your partner, it's my bet that there's an underlying relationship issue that needs to be resolved.

Let's see if we can understand what's percolating beneath the surface. How about switching our focus from all these *ideas*, to the real world. Quite simply, all I want you to do for now is identify below what the *circumstances* may be that you and your partner continually get hung up on. See if you can identify at least three *circumstances* that you and your partner go over time and time again without ever resolving. Go ahead and make a list of those circumstances.

_____
_____
_____
_____
_____
_____
_____
_____

Where There's Smoke There's Fire

Now, take a look at the list you just made and put a magnifying glass to it. What issues lay beneath the surface? Don't worry if you have a fancy label for them. Our goal right now is to create an awareness that there's more going on than a missed dinner engagement, an inability to agree on what television show to watch, or any other seemingly innocent incident that has an emotional charge to it that's out of proportion to the incident itself.

PART TWO: PINPOINTING THE ISSUE

Hopefully, things are coming together for you. Remember, the process of making molehills out of mountains is predicated on one thing and one thing only—having new choices to create more options so that you may effectively resolve the underlying issues of your relationship rather than waste your time continually trying to fix the circumstances that precipitate the conflict. The relationship skill, pinpointing the issue, is the skill that will enable you to create more choices for yourself.

I hope that the most important choice you have is more clear to you now—focus on the circumstances of the conflict or the underlying relationship issues. I hope that it's equally clear to you what is to be gained by executing that choice—staying stuck in endless frustrations, half-truths, and unspoken feelings or using the resolution of your conflict as a means to strengthen the connection between you and your partner.

In order to create the best choices possible for you, it's critical that you have a strong grasp of what the underlying issues are that live beneath the circumstances of your conflicts. The next four sections will focus on each theme of the underlying relationship issues. I will discuss with you in depth what each issue is, as well as suggest some skills that can assist you in your quest to make molehills out of mountains by pinpointing the issue.

PART 3
Acceptance

You've got to accentuate the positive, eliminate the negative, latch on to the affirmative.

-Johnny Mercer

Getting to Know You

*If I accept you where you're at, you'll become
who you are capable of being.*

-Stanley Phillips

PART THREE: ACCEPTANCE

"That cinches it," I thought to myself. "Enough is enough," I muttered under my breath as my foot pushed harder on the accelerator.

Karen and I were out for a Sunday evening drive. The top was down, it was a breezy summer evening. This was our time to be with each other, away from all the hustle and bustle that awaited us every Monday. I brought her favorite tapes along. We loved cranking up the stereo as we sang along with our favorite tunes.

However, this Sunday something was different. Karen had been quiet, somewhat withdrawn. I asked on four different occasions if anything was wrong, but she wasn't talking. In fact, she had been that way for at least a week now. Her *flavor of the week* charity dinner—she canceled out on me. That was definitely not like her. Thursday and Friday when I called to say good-night, all I got was the answering machine. My messages went unreturned. Something was definitely up, only she wasn't talking.

But there was no denying this. I turned the volume up as Carly Simon began singing *"I haven't got time for the pain. I haven't the room for the pain. I haven't the need for the pain."* Karen would always, always, sing along with Carly, almost as if the two of them were having their own private celebration about the emotional exorcisms they had undergone. But she was just sitting there, arms crossed against her chest, blankly staring off into the distance.

"Come on Kare', there's gotta be something bothering you. What is it?" I pleaded with her. "You never, ever miss a chance to sing *this* song."

"Yea, well I'm not singing anymore," she sneered at me.

"Whataya mean, you're not singing anymore?" I asked somewhat confused. "You love to sing. How can you just decide not to sing?"

"Let me be more specific then. I'm never, ever going to sing in front of you, Einstein," she said, each word dripping with sarcasm.

"Oh, why are you honoring me as the one person who you'll never, ever sing in front of?"

She turned towards me, glared and said, "Because!"

"Because why?"

"Because of what you said to me last week."

Ah, now the pieces were starting to come together. The canceled dinner. The unreturned phone calls. The silent treatment. I could see I was being punished, but I hadn't a clue as to what for.

"You have an advantage over me. I don't remember *all* that I said to you last week."

"Think hard, buddy. I have no problem remembering. Do you remember anything you said about me 'breaking a stereotype?'"

I could feel my face turn red. I sank a little in the seat as that particular conversation came flooding back to me. But I had a position to maintain here and, by god, I was sticking to it. "Honey, honestly, I don't remember. Let's just forget about it. I'm sure it's water under the bridge by now," I said, feeling somewhat satisfied that I had come up with a solution that would put an end to all of this nonsense.

But that wasn't working, because now she was ready to talk about it. "Listen, Kreskin, all of a sudden your memory doesn't work? I don't buy that. Let's see if I can refresh it for you."

PART THREE: ACCEPTANCE

I wasn't expecting her next move, she actually went into her purse and pulled out a piece of paper.

"Does this ring a bell?" she asked as she began to read from the paper. "You said, 'Karen, you've broken a stereotype that I have about all women being able to sing, because you sure can't sing.'" With that said, she balled the paper up and threw it out the window.

I knew I had to think fast. How could I spin this just a little to my advantage? Why with any luck, I might be able to get her to apologize to me for overreacting. "Okay, here goes nothing," I thought to myself.

"What's so bad about that? Up until last week, I believed that all women could sing. Is that so disparaging against you and your sisters? Come on, let's just drop it." I looked out of the corner of my eye to see how that was playing. She wasn't buying it.

"I think you're missing the point, as usual. Why do I always have to spell things out for you? You inferred that I can't sing."

"Okay, time for a tactical switch here," I thought to myself. If I couldn't go around her I was going to go over her. I tried to give her an easy way out, but she was making me do it her way.

"Karen, now that's where you have it all wrong. I didn't infer that you couldn't sing. I'm telling you right now to your face. You *cannot* sing. No *ifs, ands,* or *buts* about it. You ain't no Streisand, kid!"

"Ah ha!" she shouted.

"Ah ha, *what?*" I replied. "Is that such a crime to say to you? What's the big deal?"

I had her back-pedaling now, so I thought this was the perfect time to do what I do best, turn the tables on her, make her out to be the bad guy, show her how I'm the victim, how dare she try and make me wrong for just speaking my mind about how tone-deaf she was.

"You've been punishing me all week because I was kind enough to tell you the truth, how dare you! I'll tell you what, I will graciously accept your apology and we won't talk about this any more." I leaned over to kiss her, but she pulled away as she pushed me back to my side of the car."

"Not so quick, buster. This isn't about you. It's about how your comment made me feel."

"What do you mean *made you feel?* You can't sing! How do you think that makes me feel?"

"Steven, can we get off the singing for a moment? This isn't about my singing. It's about how your insensitive comment hurt my feelings."

"Why are your feelings hurt? I'm right about this. You *cannot,* I repeat, *not,* no how, in any way, sing."

"Forget the G.D. singing! Will you focus on me? Can you quit defending yourself long enough to hear what I'm saying? You hurt my feelings. I felt judged by you. When I feel like you're judging me, it makes it unsafe for me to be around you. I know in my head that you love me, but I feel in my heart that you don't accept me. When I feel like you don't accept me, it makes it hard for me to want to be with you."

"All of that because you can't sing?" I feigned bewilderment.

"Steven, I'm going to give you the benefit of the doubt here. You're too smart to think that this is all because you *believe* that I can't sing.

"I need to feel accepted by you. People who love each

PART THREE: ACCEPTANCE

other don't judge each other. I feel safest with you when I feel like you're on my side. I don't need to be teased by you, or belittled by you. I need to know that you accept me with all my quirks. I don't want to have to be worrying about every little thing I do and say. Should I always have to question whether you're judging me, that you're going to make fun of me? I need to know that I can just be myself around you without giving you material for your standup routine."

"Ohhh, so *that's why* you've been so angry with me all week."

I knew I had no way out of this. I could see that it was about time for me to punt. Sometimes it's better to retreat in order to live to fight another day. I'm nothing if not a gracious loser. So I did what any man would do when he's backed into a corner with nowhere else to go. I pulled the car over to the side of the road. I gave her a hug, kissed her on the cheek and said, "You are right. I am sorry. It will never happen again."

The look on each of our faces said it best, "Yea right, it will never happen again."

Man. Woman. Child. Adult. Doesn't matter your station in life. Competent. Incompetent. Bright. Not-so bright. Aloof. Sociable. Kind. Self-centered. Self-denying. Underneath all the exteriors a person can don, we're all sensitive, oftentimes frail. What we're sensitive about may vary from person to person. But make no mistake about it, we all desperately want to feel accepted by the people in our lives.

We share together the need to feel accepted. Don't buy into the assertion that there are fundamental differences between people. We are all from planet Earth.

There are fundamental truisms about human nature that apply to each and everyone of us alike. Your ability to create a harmonious relationship is dependent upon embracing one simple truism. Not operating from this space in your heart will handicap your best intentions. Overlooking this simple truism will keep you running round and round in circles with your partner, never getting to the heart of the matter.

This next sentence needs to be underlined, place an asterisk by it, write it fifty times on a blackboard. *We are much more similar than we are different.* I want to repeat that. There are profound implications for this sentence. Do not be seduced by the simplicity of this statement. *We are much more similar than we are different.*

You get it? We're all wired the same. The only difference is that some of us choose to insulate ourselves to a greater or lesser extent from all the ways we hurt, from daring to want and need. Make sense to you? You have your own level of comfort with feeling vulnerable, so you insulate yourself from the discomfort that accompanies feeling vulnerable. That, my friend, is the only difference.

Any of this sound familiar? "I don't care what anybody thinks about me?" "I'm my own person, I don't need you or anyone else." Nay. Nay. Don't believe it about yourself or anybody else.

The need for acceptance bubbles underneath the surface of any interaction you have with another human being. You may feign indifference. Or you may have made acceptance the lord of your existence. Or perhaps you have found some middle ground. But it's there. Getting stepped on. Being titillated. Spreading warmth throughout our being.

PART THREE: ACCEPTANCE

You know what it feels like, all that fear when confronted with all the firsts in your life—first day on a new job, a first date, all those first days at school. New worlds, new people, new arenas where you have to make your way. All the questioning, self-doubts. Do I belong here? Will I be liked? Will I be noticed?

You long for a kind word, a knowing nod. Remember those times someone placed a comforting hand on your shoulder? The gentle touch, a thoughtful comment, someone's willingness to go out of their way to acknowledge you and your discomfort. Fear melts away as we feel safe and accepted.

And when we don't feel safe and accepted, there are going to be hurt feelings. Not feeling accepted coats us with a thin film of alienation. Insensitive comments, myopic behavior that insures our well-being at the expense of our partner creates layer and layer of hurt, resentment, and mistrust.

I'd be willing to bet if you took the time to step back from the devices you and your partner use to hurt each other, you would learn a thing or two. If you peel back the layers to your discord, perhaps you'll discover what you and your partner are truly feuding over. The significance of how well you can sing, or dance, or make love? Perhaps that's the circumstance, but I'd be willing to bet that someone is not feeling accepted. Might this be true?

Perhaps there's a place in you that is aching from the accumulation of slights, innuendo, accusations, omissions of recognition, sarcastic observations, and more. Has your need to feel accepted by your partner been frustrated to the point that your hurt has been twisted into anger and resentment?

This is really very simple. No sophisticated psychology is needed. I'm talking about the tenderness of the human condition, the soft underbelly of the hard exteriors we create. When that underbelly is pierced, we hurt and we don't forget—it's just one more incident added to a long list. When our tenderness is honored, we don't forget that either. A little more of who we are is able to come out, delivering kindness to our partner, thereby expanding the presence of love and respect between two people.

I have no fancy techniques to offer you, only encouragement. The solution itself is seemingly easy. Stop focusing on the circumstances. Don't settle for believing that how well somebody sings is at the heart of what is troubling the two of you. Pull back and go deeper. Pull back from the battle. Go to a deeper layer and focus on the underlying hurt you're experiencing.

This is the path to a deeper appreciation of your partner. A deeper appreciation of your partner is the path to a less conflictual relationship. Less conflict needing to be resolved frees up more energy to invest in the well-being of your partner and, ultimately, the nourishment of your relationship. Afterall, isn't that why we all want to learn how to make molehills out of mountains?

Tranforming Judgments into Acceptance

In the sick room, ten cents' worth of human understanding equals ten dollars worth of medical science.

-Martin H. Fischer

PART THREE: ACCEPTANCE

Bridge-Builder's Tip

The path to accepting your partner is paved by the efforts you make to understand your partner.

What's at the core of the act of acceptance? Think about this for a moment. Is your partner more likely to want to feel that you understand them or that you're judging them? Understand or judge? What's at the root of either of those two postures?

Judging someone is easy enough to do. You have your own standards for the way a person *should* act, think, or feel. You have your own sense of what's right or wrong. Does your partner measure up to those standards? When your partner doesn't meet those standards, how do you react to that? How do you reconcile the difference between who you believe your partner *should* be and who they *are*? Isn't that really the essence of it?

Many of us try to fit our partner into a box. You know the saying about trying to fit a square peg into a round hole. Often that's what we do to the people in our lives. We don't see them for who they are. We see them for who we want them to be. We don't see the incredible richness that lives within them. We see them as projects in which we can mold them in a manner that makes us more comfortable with who they are.

Does that sound familiar at all? Molding. Shaping.

Cajoling. All in the name of what? Wanting to transform our partner's imperfections? Needing to appease *our* discomfort for what *we* can't tolerate? A little of each perhaps?

But let's look at it this way, at what cost does all of this take place? How does all of the energy you invest in trying to change your partner *help* your partner see the light; how does all of that effort play in your partner's head?

You call it being helpful. Your partner calls it being intrusive, undermining, non-accepting. You call it wanting the best for your partner. Your partner calls it not accepting them for where they're at. You call it taking an interest in your partner's life. Your partner calls it not having faith in their ability to go it alone.

All the subtle digs: a jab here, a barb there. What does the accumulation of all of that noise, all the ways we damn somebody with faint praise, what does it add up to in any relationship?

"How are you being helpful to me?" Jan asked, as tears of frustration welled up in her eyes.

"I don't know. But I don't get how you can doubt my good intentions. All I really am doing is just trying to be helpful," Alan protested.

"How does going behind me, second guessing everything I do, help me in any way, shape, or form?" Jan bitterly wondered outloud.

Alan's face was genuinely bewildered. "I'm not going behind your back. I'm merely offering an alternative for you to think about."

Jan, having lost all her patience, excitedly shouted, "Who asked you for an alternative? I don't need alternatives from you. I need your belief in me. I need your acknowledgment that you believe that I can do this, not your recommendations for how you would do it.

"Don't you know how it makes me feel like such a nothing every time you stick your nose into my business? Can't you see how belittling it is to me, to have you pick away at every little thing I do? What do you think I am? A fool? An incompetent?"

By now Jan's face was crimson red. Her arms were slicing through the air with each point she made. She continued, "You know, sometimes I think *you need* to hold it in your head that I'm somehow not capable, that I'm helpless, that I *need* you. I want you in my life, but not at this expense. I need you, but not the way you have it set up. It makes me feel judged. It makes me feel like the only way you want me is if I'm not me—but rather what you try and shape me to be."

Isn't it time for you to better understand how your helpfulness is experienced by your partner? Isn't it time for you to better understand how the *innocent* comments you make may be heard very differently by somebody else?

I can't tell you how much discord can be alleviated between you and your partner when you better understand how your best intentions are heard by somebody else. Your willingness to be better sensitized to how your partner is affected by some of the things you do and say will go a long way to helping your partner feel more accepted by you.

Understanding on the other hand is such a different game to play. The players are cast as equals. The nature of the relationship is built upon support and caring rather

Transforming Judgments into Acceptance

than correcting and fixing. You tell me, which energy nurtures your soul—fixing or understanding?

When you take the time to understand your partner, you offer an incredible gift. Do you see that?

How best to communicate this special gift? Understand your partner by *entering their world*, not by *imposing your world* upon them. Make it *safe* for your partner to introduce new pieces of who they are. Don't *censure* them for what they do and say. These are the baby steps we must take as we build a bridge of understanding. These thousand small acts of kindness and appreciation are what affirms and encourages your partner to *be* who they are.

My best friend Stephanie Phillips knows how good it feels when I understand her. Believe me it's not always easy for me. You see she's only three, so it's hard for me to crack her code all the time. But in the end, she lets me know whether I get it right or not.

"Frischie, Frischie, I 'frowd up, I 'frowd up," Stephie said as she came running to greet me.

"What's the matter, Steph, don't you feel well?" I asked as I placed my hand on her forehead.

She didn't answer, but the tears in her eyes said more than her words ever could.

"Does your tummy hurt?" I asked.

She nodded her head as she gave a little whimper.

"You wanna sit on my lap, Stephie?" I asked.

No words, she just jumped into my lap.

"Steph, you want me to rub your tummy for you?"

She nodded her head as she wiped a tear from her eye.

"How 'bout I get ya a little Coca Cola™, to settle your stomach?"

PART THREE: ACCEPTANCE

Her face brightened as she said, "'Kay!"

After Stephanie finished the Coca Cola, I layed a pillow down on the couch and held out her blanket. "Steph, you wanna lay down with your blankie?"

She nodded yes, ran over to me, threw her little arms around my neck and planted a big kiss on my cheek.

I thanked her and kissed her back. For me, it doesn't get any better than that.

I hope you're beginning to see how acceptance grows wherever seeds of understanding are planted. Acceptance is choked wherever weeds of judgment become overgrown. Having built a case for the importance of understanding, let me give you some concrete tools that will never let you down. These tools will enable you to listen to your partner in a special way; more importantly, you'll discover how to effectively respond to your partner rather than react to them. The following's a simple formula to follow—one part attitude, two parts action.

Let's deal with attitude first—the attitude you project towards your partner. Don't blow by this question. I want you to think about it for a moment or two. Do you give your partner the space to be who they are? Are there parts of who your partner is that you judge to be less than worthy of your honor and respect?

Don't fall into your 'yea but' shtick. I don't want to hear how you rationalize it in your head. How 'it's for their own good.' Or 'I know what's best.' A million times I've heard how somebody is 'only trying to be helpful.'

In your being helpful, do you insist that your partner stop being who they are? This is the essential question. Stop being emotional. Stop being frightened. Stop being irrational. Stop being obsessive. Stop being lazy.

Being judgmental, being critical—so many of us have become adept at hiding our judgments in our good intentions, in our well-meaning behavior. But don't settle for that any longer. I guarantee you that your partner doesn't.

The time has come to work *with* your partner. What that means for the purposes of this section is to *check it out* with your partner. Ask them how your attitude towards them may imply that they have to stop being who they are. See for yourself how you may be implying in many of your behaviors and comments that your partner is less than, that somehow, someway they need you to show them the way.

Ask them if they experience many of your comments as *just kidding*. Or do they feel the sting of your sarcasm, the harshness of your jokes, the cruelty of your *just being honest*? Is it possible that your partner doesn't feel accepted by you—and rightly so?

If you truly want things to be different, then it starts with you. It starts with you *getting honest* about yourself as well as what you want for your partner. Are you ready to stop minimizing the aches and pains that your partner expresses to you? Are you ready to let go of the explanations you've invented to justify your behavior to yourself and the rest of the world? If you're ready to get honest about your displaced anger, your veiled attempts at control, your misguided attempts at being helpful, let me introduce you to two action steps that will instantly transform your relationships.

Walking a Mile in Your Partner's Shoes

*The love of our neighbor in all its fullness
simply means being able to say to him,
"What are you going through?"*

-Simone Weil

PART THREE: ACCEPTANCE

Bridge-Builder's Tip

Acceptance grows from understanding how your partner experiences life through their eyes.

The first action step is *empathy*. This one step can do much to alleviate the conflict in any of your relationships. Empathy is a specific relationship skill where you choose to understand your partner by being able to see their world *as they experience it,* without judging or correcting their perceptions. So easy for me to say, so hard for any of us to do. But believe me, there's a huge payoff for your practice and patience.

I'm sure you're thinking to yourself, "What about me, what about how I see the world, what about my best interests?" I promise you, when you make the shift we're discussing, you'll discover how your best interests will be honored in ways that you never dreamt possible.

Your best interests in any relationship relies on one thing and one thing only—being able to communicate to your partner that you understand them. Your partner doesn't want to be argued with, your partner doesn't want to be corrected, your partner doesn't want to be made out to be wrong.

Do you know what your partner wants most out of life? Your partner wants to be *understood* in order that they may feel *accepted* by you. The payoff is tremendous, believe me. You'll minimize conflict, deepen the bond between you and your partner, and create a freely giving relationship.

What does empathy look like, and more importantly how does it affect your partner? Consider this scenario...

"Bobby, what's the matter? You've been moping around all day." Rhonda asked.

"There's nothing wrong with me, would you quit bugging me," Bobby snapped back.

"Come on, Bobby, can't we at least talk about it?" Rhonda pleaded.

"Talk about what? How you completely embarrassed me in front of my friends?"

"I did what? I embarrassed you in front of your friends!" Rhonda shouted back.

"Yea, you embarrassed me," Bobby said.

"How, pray tell, did I do that?" Rhonda asked as she rolled her eyes.

"You went off on me in front of Tom and Matthew," Bobby said.

"Of course I did. Don't you think I was entitled to my reaction? I'm tired of the three of you laying around here leaving a mess for me to pick up."

"Yea, Rhonda, you always have a great argument ready for me, but that's not the point. You didn't have to do it in front of them. Why couldn't we discuss it later? I've told you time and time again that I don't want you talking to me like that in front of my friends."

"And I've told you time and time again, I don't want your friends over here trashing the house," Rhonda countered.

"Whatever, but believe me, this better be the last time you pull a stunt like that in front of my friends."

PART THREE: ACCEPTANCE

What's going on here? Two people are locked in a battle of wits over who's position is more justifiable. The goal of this conversation is to build a case to justify how *wronged* each feels rather than working at understanding each other.

Empathy is an act of understanding—in this case, how a person is affected by another person's actions. Do you see how Rhonda and Bobby violated the spirit of empathy? They put their energy into forcing their own interpretation of their experiences upon each other.

My point is, as you make small shifts in how you discuss things with your partner, there will be dramatic differences in the outcome. The shift: going from being argumentative to empathetic. For instance...

"Bobby, what's the matter? You've been moping around all day." Rhonda asked.

"There's nothing wrong with me, would you quit bugging me," Bobby snapped back.

"Come on, Bobby, can't we at least talk about it?" Rhonda pleaded.

"Talk about what? How you completely embarrassed me in front of my friends?"

"I hadn't realized I embarrassed you, can you tell me how I embarrassed you?" Rhonda asked.

"It's embarrassing to have you come in and keep reminding me to clean up. You're not my mother, you know," Bobby said.

"Yes, I realize that I'm not your mother. What I didn't realize is that I was embarrassing you or treating you like your mother. I can certainly understand how that must anger you.

"But Bobby, is there some way you and I can work

together on keeping the house cleaner? I don't want to embarrass you. I don't want to nag you. But I don't think you realize how hard it is on me to keep doing this by myself."

"No, I guess I don't. You hadn't said anything to me before. What's the matter?" Bobby asked.

"It's not that there's any *one* thing that's wrong. I'm just feeling overwhelmed with a lot of different things right now. You know I like having Tom and Matthew over, but by the time the card game is over, you've got all those beer cans laying around, cigarettes all over the place, and the food just sits. It's just getting to be too much for me."

"Alright, I get your point. I hadn't realized things had gotten so out of hand. I see why you would resent what's been going on lately, how you feel like we're not working together. I know how I feel when it feels like I'm in this all alone. I don't need much imagination to figure out what you're going through now. I'm sorry. I didn't realize it earlier, but thanks for letting me know."

Do you see the difference an empathetic gesture makes? When you work at seeing things through the eyes of your partner, you take defensiveness out of the relationship and replace it with kindness, understanding, and cooperation. Empathy simply is a skill that enables you to build a bridge between what you perceive is going on between you and your partner and what your partner is experiencing.

Empathy is the antidote for one of the most toxic needs we all have—the need to be right. How many of you feel that it's more important to be right first, last, and always. Let me ask you a simple question, has it been worth it? Does it bring you the things that you claim you want?

Well, if you're ready to surrender the need to be right and make your partner wrong, then you're ready to see your partner's viewpoint of the world without judgment or need for correction. When you're able to do just that, you'll find your partner more open to accepting who you are as well.

I want to propose a formula to you to help you with this relationship skill. It's a four step process to help you become aware of: 1) your position; 2) your partner's position; 3) the impediment to understanding your partner; 4) creating a new understanding of your partner once you have let go of what was getting in the way of understanding your partner.

There are two keys to this formula. The first key is your willingness to see *two sides of any disagreement.* You know that saying about there being three sides to any disagreement: yours, mine, and the truth. At the core of your ability to be empathetic rather than argumentative is your ability to step outside of your own position long enough to consider how your partner is experiencing whatever it is they are experiencing.

The second key is your willingness to *let go.* Invariably in any disagreement, there's something that prevents you from looking at things through the eyes of your partner. There's something that you're holding onto within that's preventing that from taking place.

Some examples of those impediments may be pride, the need to be right, ego, or fear of giving in. But until you check-in with yourself to better understand what's preventing you from understanding your partner's world, you'll continue to be argumentative rather than empathetic.

For example...

Bruce: I've walked the dog every night for the last three weeks. It's time for you to walk the dog.

Alice: I don't want to. I told you I'm too tired to walk her so late at night.

Bruce: Well, what about me? Don't I deserve a break?

Alice: No, who ever said life's fair. You're always trying to get over on me. It's always somehow, someway unfair to you. But what about me? There's plenty of things I do, that I don't see you doing around here. It's time you started pitching in.

Let me walk you through the formula I just gave you in order to problemsolve this disagreement. Remember the goal is to see both sides of the disagreement in order to create a solution that considers both person's concerns. In seeing both sides of the disagreement, you want to be able to see what impediments you need to let go of in order to be able to create a new way of seeing the disagreement. Ultimately, you want to craft a solution based upon you and your partner's concerns.

Step 1: *Bruce's position.*
Bruce feels like he has been walking the dog too often.
Bruce believes that life should be fair.

Step 2: *Alice's position.*
Alice is too tired at night to walk the dog.
Alice believes that a couple should do everything fifty-fifty.

Step 3: *What needs to be let go of?*
For Bruce: Bruce believes that life should be fair; so he's fighting to even up the score.
For Alice: Alice fears that she'll be taken advantage of if Bruce doesn't do as much as she does.

Step 4: *A new way of thinking about the disagreement.*

Bruce: I can see how hard you work during the day. I'm sorry that you feel as if I'm trying to get over on you. I want you to believe that I'm here to help you more fairly shoulder the load.

Alice: I know it seems like you're doing everything. How about if we make a schedule whereby we switch off doing the different chores around the house?

How about if you give it a try yourself? Think about a point of disagreement that exists between you and your partner. Think about the position you take. Think about the position your partner takes. Do you know what you have to let go of in order to better understand your partner? Have you ever tried to let go of that impediment long enough to better understand your partner?

Do the following. Write down a disagreement you have with your partner.

_____
_____
_____
_____
_____

Walking a Mile in Your Partner's Shoes

Write down what your position is that you're trying to impose upon your partner.

Write down what you understand your partner's position to be.

PART THREE: ACCEPTANCE

Write down what you would have to let go of in order to better see your partner's side of the disagreement.

Write down a new way of thinking about the disagreement that honors you and your partner's concerns.

The point of being empathetic rather than argumentative is that you want to be able to construct a solution that includes both you and your partner's concerns. Any other way is not a solution but an imposition of wills. If you want to learn how to resolve your issues rather than fix them, this skill is fundamental to your success. Being able to see the world through your partner's eyes while letting go of whatever you are invested in holding onto will dramatically shift how you problemsolve with your partner. More importantly, it will change forever the outcome of those efforts.

Soothing the Open Wounds

Understanding a person does not mean condoning; it only means that one does not accuse him as if one were God or a judge placed above him.

-Erich Fromm

PART THREE: ACCEPTANCE

Bridge-Builder's Tip

Validate rather than discount who your partner is.

The second action step for creating acceptance is *validating*. Validating is the twin brother of empathy. Whereas empathy is understanding your partner by *perceiving* how your partner is affected by their life experiences, validating is *communicating* that understanding or perception to your partner.

The distinction is an important one, otherwise you may be confused by the similarities of empathy and validating. Empathy is nothing more than your willingness to see the world through the eyes of your partner rather than insisting that they see everything your way. Empathy is the process of stepping out of your viewpoint of the world and *perceiving* your partner's viewpoint. Validating is *communicating* that perception to your partner.

There's no greater gift to another person than to validate who they are as a thinking, feeling, caring human being. When I share this sentiment with people, I oftentimes get blank stares. Other times people argue the point with me. I am often asked how can I just sit there and agree with someone when I know they're dead wrong. My response is that the very question that has been asked is the number one symptom of the problem.

If your goal is to create a strong foundation with your

Soothing the Open Wounds

partner built upon acceptance and understanding, you'll find that you need to make a major shift from seeing your partner as right or wrong. Listen carefully to what I'm about to say next. Get the marker out again. Underline this. Think it through carefully. Think about all the ways you may violate the spirit of what I'm about to share with you. Imagine how your relationship might be different if you embraced the spirit of the following:

> *There's no one, let me repeat, no one on the face of this earth, who's looking to be argued out of what they think or feel.*

There's no one who will look kindly on the energy you expend in attempting to prove them wrong. I can't think of one human being who shares a part of themselves, who's hoping that you will, piece by piece, pick apart what they're sharing with you.

The only thing I know that will sustain the trust, love, and affection of another person is validating who they are and how they experience the way life affects them. That doesn't mean rubber stamping everything they say. It means communicating to them how you understand that person and what they're going through.

Let's see if I can make the act of validation come to life for you. Take your time with the following scenario I have created and see how well you can relate to what Ronnie is going through with his mom.

"I don't want to take dance lessons. I don't want to have to embarrass myself in front of everybody else," Ronnie said to his mother.

"Oh Ronnie, will you stop being so dramatic. You're

not going to embarrass yourself," his mom shouted back at him.

"I will too. You don't understand. I'm not going. I'm not going. You can't make me."

"Ronnie, I'm not going to keep having this discussion with you. You're being unreasonable. I have better things to do than listen to you go on and on about this. Give me one good reason why I shouldn't make you go."

"I told you, I don't want to embarrass myself," Ronnie said.

"You're overreacting. You're not going to embarrass yourself. There's absolutely no reason for you to think that way. Case closed. End of discussion."

What do you think about Mom's attempts to understand Ronnie? How much of Mom's approach to understanding Ronnie lives and breathes in your relationships?

Have you ever thought about this before? Where do you invest the bulk of your energy when you communicate with your partner? Making yourself right and your partner wrong? Justifying your position or understanding your partner? Demonstrating how good your memory is and how faulty your partner's interpretation of the past is? How about this one? Making your partner justify their feelings to you?

These are all the ways that we invalidate another person. These are all ways we communicate a lack of acceptance for somebody else.

Has your relationship become an Olympic sport—a never ending competition between you and your partner? Where did you learn that the point of communication was to win, to prove your partner wrong, to debate your differences rather than build bridges over the ground you share in common?

Soothing the Open Wounds

Let's see if there's anything you can learn about yourself by looking at the dance that Ronnie and his mom went through in the previous scenario. How do you think Ronnie felt at the end of his conversation with his mother?

What are the things that Mom said and did that made Ronnie feel that way?

PART THREE: ACCEPTANCE

What could mom have done differently in order to arrive at a different outcome?

_____
_____
_____
_____
_____
_____
_____
_____
_____
_____
_____
_____
_____

Now let's change the dialogue just a bit. Let's see whether the outcome changes or stays the same.

"I don't want to take dance lessons. I don't want to have to embarrass myself in front of everybody else," Ronnie said to his mother.

"Ronnie, what are you so afraid of?" Mom asked.

"I don't know what I'm doing and everyone else does," Ronnie said.

"We all feel afraid when we try something new," Mom agreed.

"Yea, but it's going to be just awful. I know I'm already awful at this. I've tried dancing in my room. I just can't get it right."

"I know how hard it is for you to try something new. Is there anything else that is frightening you about these dance lessons?"

"Well, yea. When we're at school, I know what to do.

I play with the guys and all that, but I won't know how to act at dance school."

Mom gave Ronnie a big hug as she said, "I know just what you mean. I'm not so old that I can't remember how terrified I was when I had to take my first dance lesson. I thought I was never going to be able to live through it."

"I bet you just didn't go, huh Mom?" Ronnie asked with the great hope that this might be his way out, as well.

"Well no, not exactly, sweetheart. My mother asked me what she could do to make things easier for me and we wound up striking a deal."

"A deal?" Ronnie asked, somewhat suspiciously.

"Yea, we made a deal that if I went to the first three lessons and I still didn't like it, that I wouldn't have to go back again."

"Oh, how did that work out?" Ronnie asked, his curiosity aroused.

"The first two weeks were horrible, I'm not going to lie to you. But by the third week, I felt a little more comfortable so I decided to keep going. Two years later, I met Daddy at a dance and the rest, as they say, is history."

"Mom, do you think you and I can make the same kind of deal?"

"Only if you want to, Ronnie," mom said as she leaned over to give him a hug and kiss.

Quite a different outcome, wouldn't you say? Why do you think that happened? Was Mom being sneaky, manipulative, or was something else at play here? Was Mom more effective in the second story or the first story? If so, what made her more effective?

PART THREE: ACCEPTANCE

What lessons might there be from these two stories? What shifts can you start making in your words and actions towards your partner that may wind up with them feeling less argued with and more validated by you?

Soothing the Open Wounds

Let's make the action step of validation as concrete as possible. Here's a five step process to follow. I have inserted in italics the dialogue from Ronnie and his mother that exemplifies what each specific step looks like in the previous anecdote.

Step #1: Listen to your partner in order that you may understand them rather than prepare to argue them out of their feelings.

"I don't want to take dance lessons. I don't want to have to embarrass myself in front of everybody else," Ronnie said to his mother.

"Ronnie, what are you so afraid of?" Mom asked.

"I don't know what I'm doing and everyone else does," Ronnie said.

"We all feel afraid when we try something new," Mom agreed.

Step #2: Encourage your partner to talk about what they want to express, rather than cut them off in order to have them listen to your agenda.

"Yea, but it's going to be just awful. I know I'm already awful at this. I've practiced dancing up in my room. I just can't get it right."

"I know how hard it is for you to try something new. Is there anything else that is frightening you about these dance lessons?"

"Well, yea. When we're at school, I know what to do. I play with the guys and all that, but I won't know how to act at dance school."

PART THREE: ACCEPTANCE

Step #3: Normalize the feelings being expressed rather than minimize them.

"I know how hard it is for you to try something new. Is there anything else that is frightening you about these dance lessons?"

"Well, yea. When we're at school I know what to do. I play with the guys and all that, but I won't know how to act at dance school."

Mom gave Ronnie a big hug as she said, "I know just what you mean. I'm not so old that I can't remember how terrified I was when I had to take my first dance lesson. I thought I was never going to be able to live through it."

Step #4: Express to your partner what it is that you understand about the feelings they're sharing.

"Ronnie, what are you so afraid of?" Mom asked.

"I don't know what I'm doing and everyone else does," Ronnie said.

"We all feel afraid when we try something new," Mom agreed.

Step #5: Express your willingness to support them.

"Mom, do you think you and I can make the same kind of deal?"

"Only if you want to, Ronnie," Mom said as she leaned over to give him a hug and a kiss.

I hope you take the time to think about the action steps of acceptance. There's much to be gained from making the shifts I've suggested to you. So many of the wounds that exist between you and your partner can be healed by simply taking the time to understand each other's point of view. But more than healing the wounds that presently exist, these action steps will do much to enrich the bond of emotional intimacy. After all, what greater gift can you give to yourself and your partner?

PART 4
Unmet Emotional Needs

My creed is that: Happiness is the only good.
The place to be happy is here. The time to be happy is
now. The way to be happy is to make others so.

-Robert G. Ingersoll

We Give In Order That We May Receive

If my hands are fully occupied in holding on to something, I can neither give nor receive.

-Dorothee Solle

PART FOUR: UNMET EMOTIONAL NEEDS

A second theme that runs deep beneath the surface of the circumstances of your conflict is your unfulfilled *emotional needs*. Our emotional needs are the heart and soul of what brings two people together. When your relationship is working for you, rest assured that your needs are getting met. When you feel like you're stuck in a web of conflict and emotional distance, it's likely that either you or your partner is feeling depleted—that in part or in whole, the source of the conflict is some emotional need going unfulfilled.

Have you ever thought about the pain that's beneath all the *noise* that gets stirred up between you and your partner? Have you ever made the connection between your unfulfilled emotional needs and the level of noise that's present in your relationship? It's sad, but true. So much of what precipitates conflict between two people is really a smokescreen for the pain that two people feel when their needs aren't getting met.

I was doing an interview on the radio recently. It was the kind of show where listeners called in and asked me questions about their relationships. One woman, Mary, called with a question about her extramarital affair...

"Dr. Frisch, how come I don't feel at all guilty about the affair I'm having?"

"Perhaps you feel justified in having the affair in the first place," I suggested.

"Absolutely!" Mary said rather pointedly.

"And is anger the only thing you feel towards your

husband right now?"

"Doctor, I've been furious with him for years," Mary replied.

"So, Mary, is this affair your way at getting back at him?" I wondered out loud.

"The no good S.O.B. deserves it. After all he's put me through, he deserves what he's got coming to him."

"Mary, it sounds like you've been through a lot with your husband," I responded.

"Doctor, you don't know the half of it. He's had at least five affairs that I know of in the last four years. Why twice I've caught him in my own bed with another woman."

"You must feel betrayed by your husband," I said.

"You're damn right I do. But it's much more than betrayal. It's all the ways he ignores me. He never wants to spend time with me. For years, I've felt like I have to beg him to pay the least bit of attention to me. At least the man I'm with now pays attention to me. I don't have to act like a lap dog just to get him to notice me."

"So you're finally getting some affection from a man?" I asked.

"You know, I hadn't thought about it that way, but you're right. When my husband and I first met, I always felt so cared for. There wasn't anything that he wouldn't do for me, but that stopped a long time ago. Back then, I felt important, like he cared about me. But now it seems like I have to go elsewhere for all that."

"Let's look at it this way then. What is it that you're getting from this other man? It's easy to see that a part of you is wanting to punish your husband for the times he has cheated on you. But it seems to me that there must be some other void that this affair is filling for you."

"It's like I said, I don't have to beg for attention. This guy makes me feel like I matter, like I count. With my husband, I've always felt, well, invisible is the best way to put it. I mean, I swear, I feel like I'm no more than a piece of furniture to him, disposable at that.

"But with my gentleman friend, I feel like he's there because of me, that he's interested in me. And because of that, I feel like I'm alive again."

"Mary, what do you mean about feeling alive again?" I asked.

"Do you know what you have to do to yourself when you are ignored for so many years? Do you know how you have to deaden yourself on the inside in order to numb the pain enough to simply get through the day? I've spent years feeling like a piece of dried out driftwood. There's only so much aching, so much unfulfilled longing that I could endure. The only way I could cope with it all, was just by deadening myself.

"Do I feel bad about this affair? No way. For the first time in years I finally feel alive."

Sadly, this is true for most of us: the choice we make is to ignore much of what's taking place rather than risk the confrontation that could make things different. We ignore our partner's behavior. We ignore our emotional longings. Our feelings shut down, we don blinders to our partner's actions, and sadly we deny our needs. Where once there was love and compassion, there remains only smoldering hostility that becomes masked by indifference and apathy.

You could hear all of this in Mary's story. The longer Mary talked, the more her emotions shifted. Initially, she

We Give In Order That We May Receive

was indifferent. As I poked around, trying to understand the underlying relationship issues buried beneath her extramarital affair, her indifference turned to anger and retribution. Finally, she touched upon the core of her pain—a profound sense of deprivation. For Mary, there was more than payback going on in her affair. In fact, payback was merely the *vehicle* used to express her deeper pain. Mary had been deprived for years—deprived of the one thing she wanted, forget wanted, the thing she *needed* most—she needed her emotional needs met.

Given the opportunity to talk about it, her pain came bubbling to the surface along with the needs she felt were unmet. Attention. Affection. Being noticed. Feeling cared about. Trust. Feeling safe. These are but a few of the emotional needs that each and every one of us have. And take notice, none of these can be fulfilled in a vacuum. These needs can only be fulfilled by the people who are in our life. This is why we create relationships.

Can you see how the unmet emotional needs Mary was experiencing turned her relationship inside out? Our emotional needs are at the bottom of the push and pull we experience in our relationships. There's a silent arm wrestling match that takes place between people that sounds something like...

- Honey, we need to spend more time together vs. I need some time to myself.
- You are constantly taking me for granted vs. I feel like I matter to you when you make time for me.
- I feel like you hardly know me vs. thanks for taking some time so we could catch up with each other.

PART FOUR: UNMET EMOTIONAL NEEDS

- I feel like you care more about that damn computer more than you do me vs. you're the most important person in the world to me.

And once you make the decision to talk about the pain rather than act it out, you have created an opportunity to resolve the underlying relationship issue rather than merely fix the circumstances of the problem. My friend Sylvia taught me her secret to the success of her marriage that she and her husband Duane discovered 35 years ago.

"Steve, it's just like that commercial on television, you know, that medicine for an upset stomach—that one where it says *takes a lickin but keeps on tickin.*

"No Syliva, that's for Timex™ watches, not Pepto-Bismol™."

"Oh yea, well, whatever. You get my point, don't you?"

"Can't say as I do," I responded with a perplexed look on my face.

"Duane and me, we agreed years ago, that there were two ways we could stay married to each other. Duane said to me, 'Syl,'—you know how Duane calls me Syl, 'Syl,— you know how muleheaded you are about everything. I figure we can keep bumping heads with each other for the next thirty years or we can try something different.'"

Syliva continued, "Duane went on to explain how we were squabbling about everything. He wanted to do his thing. I wanted to do mine. We never seemed to be there for each other. It was like we were two strangers sharing the same house.

"We fought constantly. Nothing ever got fixed from all our fighting. Oh sure, we were surviving all the bull that we did to each other, you know, it was never enough to break up over, but Duane's point was, don't you want more out of our marriage than just surviving how awful we can treat each other?"

"I see what you're saying," I said to Sylvia.

"I told you Mr. Big-Shot, my Duane doesn't talk much, but when he does, he usually says something mighty important."

"So how's that the secret to your marriage, what's that got to do with a Timex watch?"

"I'll give you a *for instance*. Whenever I tell Duane we need to talk, he'll act like he can't hear me, you know like he's asleep in his chair. Then I say to Duane, 'Duane, we can either talk about it or ignore it. If we ignore it, our marriage might take a *lickin but keep on tickin,* but is that what you want?'

"You see what I mean? Whenever one of us is feeling kinda down about things, whenever we need the other person, we gotta get their attention sometimes.

"In the old days, we used to fight about things without talking about things. You know how Duane likes to play all his sports, leaving me behind, or how I like to go for walks with him and he always complains he's too tired. Whenever we feel like we need something from the other, if ever we don't listen, then we just say, 'takes a lickin but keeps on tickin' and we know we better put our marriage first. We know it's time to check in with each other, to connect and see how we can better be there for each other."

Duane and Sylvia's solution makes a lot of sense. The art of making molehills out of mountains is predicated upon an appreciation for how damaging unspoken hurt can be between two people in any relationship. You can grow calluses over the original wounds, but the wound never heals. Indeed, the wound festers away, leaking its poison all over the people in your life. And the wound that runs deepest is the longing we experience when our emotional needs go unfulfilled.

Rest assured it doesn't have to stay that way for you. As always, you have choices in the matter. As I continually encourage you to believe, a little bit of know-how can go a long way to transform much of the conflict in your relationships into healing, understanding, growth, and love.

Howdy Neighbor!

Not what we give, but what we share,
for the gift without the giver is bare.

-James Russell Lowell

Bridge-Builder's Tip

Secure connections are created by inviting your partner into your world.

Volumes have been written about what I'm going to tackle in the next two chapters of this section. I don't want to oversimplify what is truly a complex subject. However, if you gain a heightened sensitivity for the two emotional needs I'm about to discuss with you, you'll soon discover that your relationships become considerably less conflictual, and more importantly, much more rewarding.

Secure connection. Emotional safety. I offer these two emotional needs as targets for you and your partner to stay focused on. When you feel things shifting in your relationship, bring your focus back to how safe and secure you feel with your partner. If you feel like the sand is moving beneath your feet, that something's amiss in your relationship, it's time to clarify for yourself how safe you're feeling. Trust me, by consistently honoring your need for a secure connection and emotional safety, most of your other emotional needs will automatically get met along the way.

Let's start with a secure connection. In my estimation, this is the most profound emotional need we have. Your relationships are the cornerstone of your emotional and spiritual well-being. They're the source of much of the emotional sustenance you depend upon in your day to day life. The more stable your connections are with the people who matter most, the more grounded and secure you'll feel.

So much of what we desire is derived from the nurturance we receive from other people. Tenderness. Caring. Affection. Belonging. We all know how good it feels to be loved and cared for. Afterall, that's why we go to all this bother in the first place. These are but a few of the emotional needs that can only be met, in part or in whole, through our involvement with other people.

Therein lies the vulnerability you experience in your relationships. You know only too well how tentative your connection to anybody can be at any point in time. Relationships are dynamic, ever-changing. The strength of your connection with your partner shifts and changes. You come together and drift apart. An intense feeling of closeness exists at one point, yet somehow that closeness can transform into the precipitant for the two of you to retreat from each other.

Other times you may experience you and your partner drifting apart, incapable or unwilling to find your way back to each other. The retreat is shrouded in the ways you have of creating, maintaining, and sustaining conflict. Yet sadly, the pain created from feeling disconnected, from feeling too far away from your partner, can all too often go untalked about. Does any of this have a ring of familiarity for you? Are there times when your emotional need to feel securely connected to your partner goes unstated as you focus on everything else but the pain of feeling disconnected?

PART FOUR: UNMET EMOTIONAL NEEDS

Let's do a reality check. Are there times that you feel like your partner's attentions, or their emotional presence has diminished or disappeared altogether? Do you recognize the feeling of trepidation, even distrust as your partner becomes more emotionally unavailable? Do you have words for the emotional undertow that tugs at you as you attempt to get your partner to emotionally reenage with you? The connection that once was so consistent, so dependable is seemingly gone, vanished into thin air.

That's what's at the core of much of the discord that you and your partner create as it relates to your emotional need for a consistent connection. As your need for a stable connection gets frustrated, the pain derived from your insatiable desire to have your partner be close and your partner's inability or unwillingness to do so bubbles beneath the surface.

How about the other side of the coin—your need to maintain a certain amount of distance and the fear that the amount of that distance stirs in your partner. Here's the point. Lurking beneath the surface of much of your conflict is the unexpressed pain created by two people doing the dance of creating a connection that carries an incredible burden. The burden? How to keep things both *safe enough* and *fulfilling enough* for two people to create and sustain emotional intimacy in their relationship.

Think of all the words we have to describe that emotional disconnect. Abandonment. Withdrawal. Retreat. Betrayal. Unavailable. Non-committal. Think of all the reasons we create to justify that disconnect. Fear. Punishment. Ignorance. Indifference. Think of all the pain that is stirred up when you feel disconnected from your partner. Isolation. Loneliness. Alienation.

These are the corrosives that eat away at our emotional and spiritual well-being. It's easy enough to see why. The emotional underbelly of feeling disconnected is discouragement, anger, resentment, and depression—an emotional state that takes on a life of its own, spiraling out of control.

But when we're grounded by stable connections with people who honor and respect ourselves, our emotional world takes on a whole different hue. For instance...

A few weeks ago a gentleman was completing the process of leaving one of my Relationship Bridge-Builders groups. When someone leaves the group, we take three weeks to say good-bye. It's important to say good-bye in a way that brings honor to all the blood, sweat, and tears that each group member has invested in building caring, nurturing relationships with each other. This gentleman was no exception. He was truly loved by each group member.

As the time was winding down in his final session, our departing group member was asked what it was he would be taking from his experience in the group.

As he thought about the question for a moment, tears began to well up in his eyes. When he finally spoke, his voice quivered as he softly said, "Family. What I have gotten most from my experience here is a sense of family.

"I never had that before. I have never known what it's like to be loved by so many good people. Learning how to get close and *stay close* to you guys has been the greatest gift to me."

He paused for a moment to collect his thoughts. The person sitting next to him offered a Kleenex. He wiped his eyes and continued. "Knowing how much you care about me, feeling free enough to be able to express it, that's meant everything to me. I carry you guys around with me wherever I go. Your words of encouragement ring in my head everytime I try something new. Your loving glances calm me whenever I'm feeling overwhelmed."

He chuckled to himself as he saw the irony in what he was about to say. "Knowing how much you care about me has empowered *me* to care about *me*. I never realized before I joined this group just how little I cared about myself, but being here with you week after week, the kindest gift of all was you letting me into your world, accepting me no matter how awful I behaved, I was able to finally accept myself, even begin to love myself."

Feeling connected means everything to us, yet sadly, we can be inept at creating and sustaining a meaningful connection. I'm going to suggest to you one simple skill. This skill will help you successfully negotiate the dance of coming together and drifting apart. This skill will cement those times when you're safely connected. It will help you find each other when you've drifted apart.

You'll scoff at me. You'll think to yourself that there has to be more to it than what I'm about to suggest. You'll accuse me of oversimplifying, underestimating the complexity of human interaction, overgeneralizing the influence of this one skill—but I promise you, in all my experience, the quality of any relationship bridge is predicated upon how well you do one thing and one thing only!

The one thing? I call it *checking-in*. Checking-in is a simple skill that enables the bond between you and your partner to grow and strengthen. It's a skill that will enable you to make your connection more and more secure.

By initiating the process of checking-in, you and your partner can create, maintain, and sustain a secure connection that will enable you to support rather than withdraw from each other.

Think of checking-in as the process of taking the temperature of yourself, your partner, and your relationship. You take the temperature by sharing something about yourself—your thoughts, feelings, and beliefs. Sharing about yourself in this very specific way creates a special bond between you and your partner—a bond that makes your connection more and more secure.

How to check-in? There's a simple skill to use when you want to check-in with your partner. I wrote about it in another of my books, *Building Better Bridges*. The fancy term for this skill is *self-disclosure*. In more simplistic terms, I refer to it as the *act of letting yourself be known to the world*. Take it from me. I sit in groups all week long. I watch people go through every gyration known to mankind. The point of all the twisting and turning? To avoid. To avoid being seen. To avoid being exposed. To avoid being found out. To avoid the intensity of a close connection.

Day after day I watch people construct a wall between themselves and the rest of the world. I watch how adept they are at creating emotional and physical distance between themselves and the people in their lives. Sadly, I bear witness to the resultant chaos they create in their lives, the bitter pain that grows out of living in a self-protected world that keeps them safe, yet shuts out the rest of the world.

But I'm never discouraged. I've also had the privilege of watching a transformation take place when a person gives up the struggle—the struggle of wanting to have great relationships without taking any risks. And the biggest risk of all, the biggest risk that has the greatest return, that risk is sharing who you are with another human being.

I must tell you, my friend, there's no avoiding this one immutable law. Your most important emotional need—feeling securely connected to your partner—is going to be fulfilled through both your *willingness* and *know-how* to open up and let your partner in.

You see we're back to that *willingness* thing and that *relationship skill* thing—*checking-in* and *self-disclosure*. Notice how we're back to that *choice* thing: shut people out or let them in.

Let's look at what happens when Mandy tries to check-in with Sydney. Notice how the lack of self-disclosure keeps a connection distant and how the presence of self-disclosure can forge a bond of love and support.

Scenario #1

"How was your day?" Mandy asked.
"Pretty much the same as usual," Sydney replied.
"That's not saying much," a frustrated Mandy said.
"There's not much to say," Sydney said.
"Well, something had to happen," Mandy said.
"No, not really. I called a few clients. Took a few

orders. Oh, yea. Now that you mention it, they let Alvin go. You remember Alvin, don't you? Been there for at least fifteen years."

"That must have been upsetting," Mandy observed.

"Upsetting? Gee, I don't know. I didn't give it much thought," Sydney said.

"Hey, by the way, did you want to rent a movie tonight?" Sydney asked Mandy.

"Syd, don't shut me out like that. I want to know what's going on with you. You must have been affected somehow, someway by Alvin being fired," an exasperated Mandy replied.

Sydney was taken aback by Mandy's insistent tone. All this did was serve to make him defensive and somewhat combative. "Shut you out, what are you talking about? You asked me how my day was. I told you. I went to work, did my thing, yada, yada, yada. Now I'm asking you, do you want to watch a video with me tonight?

"Is there something else that I'm not getting here? If so, please tell me. Otherwise get off my back. What more do you want from me? How can you accuse me of shutting you out?" Sydney asked as he walked out of the room with both eyes glued to the TV guide.

Doesn't this couple remind you of Jack Webb's character, Sergeant Friday? You know what I mean—*just the facts ma'am*. You can see why, can't you? Does this couple connect or merely exchange information?

Name, rank, and serial number. That's Sydney's *modus operandi*. Does that build bridges or walls between two people? Exchanging information is not an invitation to let your partner in, it's an act of keeping your partner out. You give your partner a lot of information but very little of you. It's really quite simple. Information is just the means used to put your partner off.

Connecting through checking-in has a very specific purpose—to build an *emotional bridge* between two people. An emotional bridge can only be constructed by letting someone into your world—not shutting them out; self-disclosure's sole role in this process is to enable you to talk *with* your partner, not *at* your partner.

But think about this for a moment. What was the purpose of Sydney's conversation with Mandy in the above scenario? Was it to share something about himself with Mandy? Was it to invite Mandy into his world so that she could better understand him? Was it to reach out to Mandy for support? And how does all of that make Mandy feel?

Take a moment and write down some lessons that Sydney might learn about how Mandy is affected when he shuts her out.

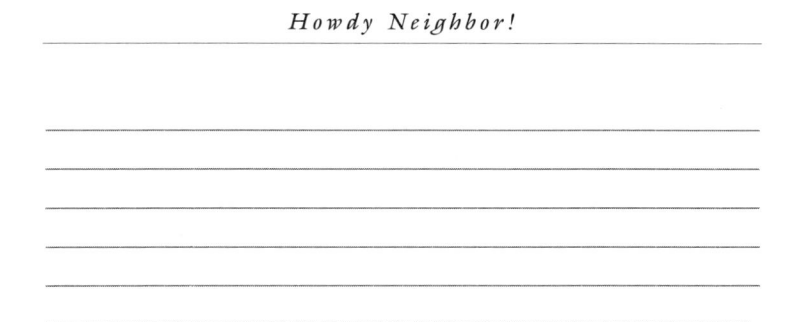

Now let's see what things look like when Sydney does more self-disclosing when Mandy checks-in. Notice how the tone changes between them. Notice how the outcome ends in support, and physical and emotional connection rather than physical and emotional abandonment.

Scenario #2

"How was your day?" Mandy asked.
"You know, did the usual. But in the afternoon, boy, work was in an uproar," Sydney replied.
"What happened?" Mandy asked
"They let Alvin go," Sydney said.
"Alvin?" Mandy asked
"Yea, you remember Alvin. Whew, that blew me away. If they'll do that to Alvin, they'll do that to anybody."
"You sound worried," Mandy said kindly.
"Yea, you know how it is out there. I can ill afford to lose my job now, yet I feel like I'm waiting for the other

PART FOUR: UNMET EMOTIONAL NEEDS

shoe to drop and I'm afraid it's going to land right on me. Can you imagine what would happen to us if I lost my job?"

"Now Syd, I understand how worried you are, but you don't have to let your imagination run wild. We'll be all right," Mandy said, trying to reassure Sydney.

"I don't know. I feel like we're both carrying such a big load as it is. I worry about the burden it will put on you. And where's someone my age going to get a job like I have now?"

"Syd, how can I reassure you? We'll both be all right."

"Mandy, just your asking helps. You know how I get when things get all bottled up. I know you'd be there for me, but hearing you say what you said, keeps my mind from racing."

"Oh yea, I know. But thanks for letting me know where you're at. I promise you, though, everything is going to be all right," Mandy said as they both hugged each other.

Do you see the difference between the second scenario and the first? Sydney was more willing to talk about himself rather than videos and television programs. In the first scenario, Sydney became defensive and walked away. In the second scenario, he willingly told Mandy how he was affected by Alvin being fired. Because he let Mandy in, she was able to be there for him rather than having to guess at what was going on with him.

Do you see how checking-in created a secure connection in scenario #2 whereas Sydney's unwillingness to check-in in scenario #1 created a wall? In scenario #2, the connection was created out of Sydney's willingness to be open by using the skill of self-disclosure.

Let's review for a moment. The skills are *checking-in* and *self-disclosure*. The act is letting someone into your world by sharing who you are with them. The means to letting someone into your world is *sharing yourself.* What you share about yourself with another person are your thoughts, feelings, and beliefs.

Checking-in as it relates to the sustaining of a secure connection between you and your partner has a very specific focus—you, your partner, the relationship, and the here-and-now. There's a lot to chew on in that last sentence. Let me pick it apart so that you can better appreciate the enormity of what I'm suggesting.

The hoped for outcome of checking-in is to keep you and your partner connected. The purpose of checking-in with each other is to demonstrate an interest and concern with how each of you are doing.

There are several benefits to inviting your partner into your world. I have already talked about how important feeling understood is. Self-disclosure is the basis for which your partner will best be able to understand you. The more open you are, the less your partner will have to guess at what is going on with you.

Feeling better understood creates a bond between you and your partner. Each new bond that's constructed between you and your partner makes your connection all that much more secure. The ultimate outcome of a more secure connection is a continued feeling of acceptance, feeling cared about, and every other goodie that we so desperately want from our relationships.

When you and your partner take the time to check-in with each other, treat it as the precious time that it is. Use it as an opportunity to focus on the state of yourselves as well as the relationship. If you're problemsolving with your partner, spend as much time on the underlying relationship issue as you do on the circumstances that created the problem.

Finally, when focusing on the underlying relationship issue, use the following guidelines as a way of talking about yourself and the relationship. You'll discover instantly what a difference the skill of checking-in will make in untangling the conflict you're experiencing, thereby strengthening your connection with your partner.

The Do's and Don'ts For Effectively Checking-in

- Talk with your partner rather than at your partner.
- Talk about yourself or the relationship rather than irrelevant external circumstances.
- Express what you need from your partner rather than relive a laundry list of past wrongs.
- Express the feelings you're experiencing in the moment rather than editorialize with your opinions and judgments.
- Focus on the here-and-now rather than the distant past or the unpredictable future.
- Share pieces about who you are rather than explain your partner to your partner.

- Share pieces about who you are rather than exchange information.
- Share pieces about who you are rather than defending or justifying who you are.

This is a skill that's going to take a lot of practice. It will feel unnatural to you at first. You will feel self-conscious, in some ways, emotionally naked.

The only way this will begin to feel more comfortable for you is to do it over and over again. By undertaking the risk of checking-in with your partner, your partner has a responsibility to you. That responsibility is to honor your efforts at creating a stronger connection with you. You see, the cement that will hold this together for the two of you is trust. You'll need to know that your partner is trustworthy—that no harm or embarrassment will come to you because of your efforts.

So take your time with this skill. You'll backslide, I guarantee it. Just know that when you pull back, it's okay to do so. But you need to understand that you're pulling back to seek cover. Once it feels safe again, commit to coming back out again.

Do you see the paradox I'm suggesting? It's a whole new way of defining what a safe relationship is. I'm suggesting a new way of creating safety for both of you. Emotional safety is no longer buried in the foxhole in which you've lived much of your life, but nestled in the safety that comes from two people being securely connected.

Becoming Captain of the Safety Patrol

*Tolerance is the oil which
takes the friction out of life.*

-Wilbert E. Scheer

PART FOUR: UNMET EMOTIONAL NEEDS

Bridge-Builder's Tip

Treat the words your partner shares with you as the precious gems that they are.

Dale's words caused Marty's body to recoil, much as if he had been struck with a bullet fired from a gun.

"That does it, I'm not doing this with you anymore," Marty shouted.

Strangely Marty's actions, the words spoken, the depth of Marty's anger, didn't seem to phase her in the least. In fact, it appeared that there was a look of satisfaction on her face, just the smallest hint of amusement in her smile.

"I mean it, Dale. I just can't keep taking this."

"Taking what?" she asked, more annoyed than curious.

"You know damn well what I'm talking about. The way you shoot me down. I feel like I go out on a limb and there you are right behind me, sawing the branch off."

"Marty, don't you think that you're being just the least bit dramatic?"

"Dramatic! You know how hard it is for me to open up to anyone in the first place. And then when I do so with you—what you do with it—it's inhumane."

"I'm not following you," Dale said in her most discounting tone.

"Follow this, why don't you! I try and tell you how I feel about you and the next thing I know, you tear into me."

"Give me an example," Dale challenged Marty.

"I don't have to prove this to you, although I can tell you this much. I know when you're doing it. I feel it in my gut. It feels like I've been kicked by a mule."

Unmoved by Marty's protest, Dale's voice became harder rather than softer. "Listen, there are times that you go too far with things. I'm just trying to let you know to cut it out."

"Letting me know is one thing, but you become downright cruel. There's no way the punishment fits the crime. You take what I say to you, twist it, distort it, ultimately you use it against me."

"That certainly is your perception of things, but it doesn't mean that I agree with you," Dale said.

"My God, Dale, I'm not asking you to agree with me. I'm asking you to understand how your actions affect me. This isn't about whether your behavior is justified or not. It's about how unsafe you make me feel. It's about how I feel like closing up like a clam after one of your slams."

"Marty, all I can hear right now is you blaming me. I want to understand you, but I don't get what you're saying," Dale explained.

"It's real simple. I consider the things I share with you to be sacred. They're like precious jewels. But you treat my words like toothpicks that you just snap in half whenever I have displeased you."

Dale started to interrupt Marty, but Marty waved Dale off.

"No, don't. Just hear me out. Opening up to you the

way I do, do you have any idea how vulnerable, how fragile I feel? And then you come along and stomp on me, it's like you are squishing the life out of a bug. It's like you have a sixth sense for what I'm feeling so vulnerable about and then you just go after it.

"I need to feel safe in order to be with you. I need to trust that you aren't going to hurt me, that you aren't going to use my words against me. Worst of all, I never know when it's going to happen. I always have to keep my guard up, I never know when you're going to pounce on me next.

"Don't you get it, Dale, the very way you protect yourself causes me to feel unsafe with you. I can't keep doing this with you if I can't feel safe."

We all have the need to feel emotionally safe with the people in our lives. If you want to create a relationship that's rewarding and fulfilling, you need to insure that both you and your partner feel safe with each other. There's no way your relationship can grow and develop without that condition being met.

Remember, a secure connection and emotional safety are the two fundamental building blocks upon which an emotionally satisfying relationship is built. By fulfilling these basic emotional needs, you'll be that much better able to have many others fulfilled.

In the last chapter, we focused on two skills, checking-in and self-disclosure. These are the fundamental skills to use in order to create a secure connection. However, you can't have a secure connection without an atmosphere of openness created by a climate of emotional safety.

Now this is easy enough to see why. The emotional nutrients of any relationship are openness and emotional honesty. Feeling emotionally safe is the primary ingredient necessary for emotional intimacy to grow and develop in your relationships. If you don't feel safe, you'll shut down, turn off, and tune out. The connection that you've worked so hard to create will shrivel up, wither away, and all too often, die.

What makes a relationship emotionally safe? Does the word *respect* make sense? Think about your own experiences. Think about the risks that you've taken with somebody. Did you feel like the risks you took were received with respect? Was there a sense of being honored for sharing something about yourself with somebody? Did you feel encouraged to continue taking risks with that person?

Trust makes a relationship emotionally safe. Trust is created out of the track record that you build with somebody. Has experience taught you that your partner works hard at understanding you? Or do your words become the tools that your partner uses to humiliate you? Using your words against you—these are the kinds of experiences that contribute to an emotionally unsafe relationship.

Taking ownership of your behavior is a third way to create an emotionally safe relationship. Taking ownership of your behavior removes the voices of blame and victimization from your relationships. In order for you to feel safe in your relationships, it's critical that you feel safe enough to be yourself without fear of blame and retribution.

Whenever there's blame being projected, nobody can feel safe. Blame makes you feel like a target. When you feel like a target, you must necessarily defend yourself. Feeling like a target, anybody will naturally defend themselves first, and build relationship bridges later.

The best way to diffuse that vicious circle is to blame less and take ownership more often. Being open to seeing your part in any dynamic with your partner enables your partner to feel much more open to seeing their part. That is the formula to resolving conflict and making things feel safe for you and your partner.

What I'm suggesting to you is the need to develop an emotional tone in your relationships. The tone expresses something special—the essence of which may seem somewhat simplistic to you. What this essence communicates is that you and your partner are for each other. Cooperation supplants competitiveness. Understanding displaces judgment. Acceptance blooms where criticism once ruled.

Whenever there is a prevailing sense of emotional safety there's a feeling of warmth and camaraderie. You feel safe in the knowledge that you have at least one person on your side wanting to be there for you rather than being against you. Life feels a little lighter, your burdens feel a little easier to bear.

Emotional safety is not something you can simply wish to have happen for you. There are things you can do to create that climate. Much of what we have discussed in earlier sections of the book are part of the puzzle. Things like acceptance, empathy, and validation. Now let me suggest more tools that will assist you in building emotionally safe relationships. Using these skills will build trust into your relationship. The presence of trust will enable the two of you to feel safe with each other in order to take more and more risks that will build an even more secure connection.

Bridge-Builder's Tool

*Use information to understand your partner,
not to use it against them.*

Laurie's face had turned a bright red. She was so embarrassed. All she wanted to do was find a hole to climb in and hide.

"I told you that in the strictest confidence," Laurie said. "How dare you bring that up again!"

"I'm just trying to prove what a hypocrite you are," Ralph said.

"A hypocrite? What's that have to do with anything?" Laurie asked.

"It has everything to do with it. All I'm saying is last week you told me all those things about you and your mom. And I can't help but think that if that is how you are with your mom, then...."

Laurie cut Ralph off before he could complete what he was about to say. "'Then,' nothing! One has absolutely nothing to do with the other.

"But I'll tell you this much. I can't believe how offended I feel. I can't believe that you would take what I told you, twist my words, and then try and apply them to a completely different set of circumstances."

"Why not? It seems like a perfectly normal thing to do. You make all these promises to me and expect me to believe you. I'm just pointing out that there's no reason to believe you, based upon what you told me about you and your mother."

By now, Laurie was more hurt than embarrassed. Tears were running down her cheeks. She couldn't believe how betrayed she felt.

"Ralph, you're missing the whole point. I told you that stuff about me and my mom, because I wanted you to better understand why it's so hard between her and me. I sure as hell didn't expect you to take that information and blow it out of proportion in every other aspect of my life."

"I'd be a fool not to," Ralph said.

"No, you're a fool for doing it," Laurie said.

"Why's that?"

"Because you're causing more damage by misusing what I told you than the damage you fear I'm going to create in the first place."

"How do you figure?" Ralph asked.

"Because I'm going to think twice before I tell you anything anymore. I don't like having to be so guarded with anybody. I'm going to resent you for what you've just done to me and I'm going to resent you for not being able to trust you in the future."

"Why can't you trust me?" Ralph asked.

"Because I don't want to have to worry about what you're going to do with something once I share it with you. When I open up to you, I'm just sharing a part of myself with you, I'm not looking to have it shoved back into my face two weeks later when it suits your purposes to do so."

The skills we have talked about in this book have one aim—diffusing conflict by *better understanding* your partner and more *effectively expressing* that understanding to your partner. Your best intentions will be defeated if all the new ways you have to express yourself are used against you.

It's a very simple proposition. You and your partner both deserve to be treated with respect as you learn how to pinpoint the issues in your relationships. You need to understand that the skills you're learning are tools of healing, not bullets to be loaded in a gun to be fired at your partner.

Healing through understanding is the goal. Don't take your sights off that target. Understanding is created through all the new ways of communicating we've talked about.

These ways of communicating are sacred. They need to be honored as such. Communication is most effective when it feels safe to express what you need to express.

Take some time to review the list I have created below. Think about how this list may enrich your relationship. Is there at least one pointer on this list that you can adapt immediately?

This list of do's and don'ts can open up doors to the people in your life. But you know, this is no instant formula to happiness. You must be willing to practice these skills and be ready for the inevitable disappointments that come with trying something new.

The Do's and Don'ts for Creating Emotional Safety

- Don't take for granted what your partner is sharing with you. It may strike you as unimportant, but don't mistake that as being true for your partner. Treat it with the respect that you would want accorded to what you might share.
- Don't twist the meaning of what's being shared with you. Check it out with your partner how you're hearing what has been said to you. Make sure you understand what your partner is trying to communicate, not what you want to understand from it.
- Don't throw information in your partner's face. Be clear that whatever your partner shares with you, it's not going to be used as ammunition against them in the future.
- Honor your partner. Let your partner express what they need to express. By not personalizing what your partner expresses, you will reduce the defensiveness that can arise from honest communication.
- Listen to your partner. Your partner is not looking to have their feelings debated. Avoid attempting to argue away or fix away somebody's feelings. Be a sounding board that affirms your partner's feelings.
- Thank your partner for taking the risks that they have taken with you. Acknowledge the importance of what you have been entrusted with. Let your partner know that you understand the risk they have taken.

Bridge-Builder's Tool

Heal the hurts in your relationships rather than store them up as ammunition.

"All right, that's enough already!" Pat said angrily.

"Enough! I'm just getting warmed up," Barb said.

"Stop it, won't you?" Pat pleaded.

"Oh, you think I should go easy on you now?" Barb asked.

"Yea, don't you think I've been through enough?" Pat reasoned.

"You think you should get a free ride just because you quit drinking? What do you think I've been through the last fifteen years?"

"I know what you've been through, Barb. You've been telling me nonstop now for the last three hours," Pat said.

"You don't think I'm entitled to blow off some steam? I had to watch what I said when you were drinking because I didn't want to set you off. Now you're saying you're too frail to take responsibility for the things you did to me?"

"No, I'm not saying I'm frail. I'm saying it's unfair to keep beating me over the head for every crime I committed. What good is it going to do either of us to keep citing me chapter and verse about every last thing that I've done to you?" Pat asked.

"It makes me feel better," Barb shouted.

"I'm glad it works for you, but it makes me feel like crap," Pat said.

"I'm tired of worrying about your feelings. When are you going to start worrying about mine?" Barb asked.

"I can't possibly begin to do that until you stop launching these missiles at me. If I didn't have to dodge every misdeed I've done, then perhaps I could start thinking about you and your feelings."

I call it *laundry listing*. Keeping track of all the slights you have suffered at the hands of your partner, never shy of reminding them about the sins they've committed.

But laundry listing is merely a device that fans the flames of conflict rather than makes molehills out of mountains. I'm not saying that you aren't entitled to feel hurt or angry or betrayed. I'm merely asking how does clinging to your laundry list serve the overall well-being of your relationship?

That's why resolution is so important. Think of all the unresolved issues in your relationship as jagged edges that you and your partner continually trip over. How does it feel to have those jagged edges tossed around, days, weeks, even months after the crime was committed?

Part of resolving conflict means that you have to let go of the past as you move towards living in the here-and-now. How do you practically let go of the past? In a word, forgiveness. If your goal is to create a climate of emotional safety, forgiveness is the final stop to that destination.

There's no getting past this ultimate truism. Making molehills out of mountains is one part awareness of the underlying relationship issue, one part effectively communicating that awareness with your partner, one part letting go of your hurt and anger, and one part forgiveness.

Can you see how important forgiveness is in the equation? Do you recognize how you have a tendency to hold onto the hurts and slights that have come your way? Do you keep track of them, constantly replaying them in your head, throwing them up in your partner's face from time to time?

What prevents you from letting go of feeling *wronged*? Is forgiveness a place you want to wind up with your partner as you work through the issues in your relationships? There are many people who choose to live in the energy of their hurt and pain. Many people I work with choose— that's right it's a choice—to stay hurt, to feel wronged rather than forgive.

The choice is a simple one. Live in the energy of self-righteous indignation or the energy of forgiveness. Self-righteous indignation perpetuates the cycle of wounding, whereas forgiveness heals. Self-righteous indignation creates pseudo-power for the wronged, forgiveness empowers both parties. Self-righteous indignation widens the split between two people, forgiveness forges a bond of caring and intimacy.

How does that last paragraph fit for you? Can you identify at least once in your life where you chose to cling to the energy of self-righteous indignation rather than grow into an energy of forgiveness? Let's walk through this step by step. Let's see if we can identify what keeps you stuck in your hurt, anger, and resentment. Just what will you need to let go of in order to create an energy of forgiveness?

PART FOUR: UNMET EMOTIONAL NEEDS

What is your laundry list of grievances that you keep alive?

_____
_____
_____
_____
_____
_____
_____
_____
_____
_____
_____

What do you gain by continually bringing them up to your partner? What do you fear that you'll lose if you let go of them?

_____
_____
_____
_____
_____
_____
_____
_____
_____
_____
_____

Let's rearrange your laundry list. Take the items on the list from above and write them down below in the following order. Rank in order, from easiest to hardest, those items that you are ready to forgive your partner for. Number one on this new list would be the item that you are most comfortable transforming from anger and resentment into forgiveness. The last item on the list would be the one transgression you absolutely refuse to forgive your partner for. This list is your blueprint to start letting go of those hurts you are ready to let go of.

Hopefully, you're starting to see your choices for how safe or unsafe you can make your relationship. You have the power within you to create a climate of forgiveness or a climate of retribution. You have the power to create a climate of kindness and understanding or a climate of belittlement and ridicule.

You have an enormous opportunity to empower your partner to join you in your efforts to create a relationship that is built upon a foundation of emotional safety. Don't be seduced by the allure of revenge. Revenge is a mirage that embitters rather than resolves. Creating a climate that's safe between you and your partner is hard work. But it's a critical element to sustaining the well-being of your relationship.

Don't sell emotional safety short. You have a *right* to experience it with all the people in your life. You have an *obligation* to create it with whomever you build a relationship bridge with.

PART 5
Appreciation

*The deepest principle in human nature
is the craving to be appreciated.*

-William James

The Magical Elixir

Wise men appreciate all men, for they see the good in each and know how hard it is to make anything good.

-Baltasar Gracian

PART FIVE: APPRECIATION

She tried hard to fight back her tears. As her chin quivered, she absent-mindedly rubbed her hands. It was as if she were trying to exorcise every last emotion from her being. The hurt and anger burned white hot in her belly. As she laid in bed, feeling beaten down one more time, she reflected upon the years of futility they had put her through.

Her whole life, she had endured the pain of being discounted. Her feelings, thoughts, and beliefs, all the times she tried to exercise her own choices, washed away in a sea of *kindness* that communicated the cruelest message of all, "I know what's best for you."

All those times. She wanted so desperately to just once receive a knowing nod, a kind word, a look of support rather than that G.D. frown. Oh that frown said it all. "I only want what's best for you, dear." Somehow that sentiment implied "I'm the only living authority on that subject." That frown seemed to be a license to meddle, to undermine, to rob her of every sense of individuality that she possessed. That damn frown gave a whole new meaning to that once innocent sentiment, *Father Knows Best.*

Just once she would like to be appreciated for who she was, not what they had tried to mold her into being. Couldn't they see it, accept it? Why couldn't they honor her? It was as if she were invisible. Yet, she didn't know how to fight back.

Self-doubt. Self-loathing. Toxic shame. The war waged on inside of her, the war that tears a child apart when she's torn between wanting to win her parent's love and approval and honor her own desire to be appreciated as a separate adult of value and worth.

The fight always took so much out of her. Standing up to them; afterall, maybe they were right. Whereas you and I look to our parents to provide the emotional sustenance to help create our sense of self, all she got were the toxic double messages that implied, "We will only appreciate you if...."

And so she waged the war that expressed her pain in a hundred different ways, but never resolved the issues between her and her parents. She drank *at them*. Used cocaine *at them*. Sexed *at them*. Last month, she had her third abortion *at them*.

It was the only way she knew how to fight back. It was the only way to break through the deafening silence, the subtle judgments, the crushing blindness.

How could they be so blind to what they were doing to her? The weight of her unexpressed anger made her spirit bow much as if it were an anvil crushing her shoulders. Beneath that anger oozed the hurt from a wound rubbed raw from years of feeling unappreciated, unrecognized, quite simply not valued.

Recognition. Appreciation. Feeling valued. That's the battlefield upon which much conflict is waged between two people. There's nothing so tender as our longing to be appreciated by the people in our lives. Whether it's our actions or our sense of self, we feel so much better when somebody acknowledges the value they hold us in.

I told you about my friend Stephanie Phillips. She has an older sister, Abby. Abby taught me a lesson about how empowering it is for her when I let her know that she's

PART FIVE: APPRECIATION

worth my time and consideration to help her become who she wants to be.

Last week Abby and I were playing basketball. She was frustrated by the limitations that her age and size imposed on her. She let me know in no uncertain terms that she didn't want to play ever again. So we sat down and talked about what was troubling her.

"I don't want to play anymore, Frischie," Abby adamantly declared.

"Why not?" I asked.

"It's too hard. I just can't make a basket."

"You know, Abby, when I watch you play, I can see how much talent you have for the game, but I know what it's like to feel so discouraged. Would you mind if I tried to help you a little?"

"Really, Frischie, you really think that I'll be able to learn how to play better?" Abby asked, somewhat hopefully.

"Abby, there's no question in my mind. I know it's hard for you to see right now. But if that's what you want, then I want to help you all I can."

"How can you help me?"

"Well, we could practice together, a couple times a week. I can give you some pointers."

"Really? You mean it, Frischie, just you and me? You'd really do that with me?" Abby asked. Her eyes were as big as saucers.

"Absolutely, Ab'. If that's what you want. You're worth it to me."

Feeling appreciated is a tonic for much of what discourages us in our lives. However, sadly enough, in many relationships, appreciation is often held hostage to pettiness and spite. Is your relationship a celebration of who your partner is or a never ending chorus of what they are not? It's as simple as the age old question, is the cup half-empty or half-full?

Think about this. Do you dwell on honoring your partner or bemoaning how they have disappointed you? Does your sense of entitlement and self-indulgence override your willingness to honor your partner?

When your urge to withhold overrides your willingness to acknowledge your partner, how does that impact your partner? What does it stir within anyone's soul when they are feeling unappreciated? Most importantly, how do those feelings impact the well-being of your relationship?

How many of us give voice to that ache, our never ending desire to be acknowledged, to be recognized for the person we are and the things that we do? It's such a simple word, appreciation. Yet, it's a sentiment that gets buried in the smoldering resentments, all the unfulfilled needs, the unmet expectations, and the buried fantasies that can overwhelm any of our relationships.

Is there a connection for you between unvoiced disappointments, hurt never expressed, buried feelings from your partner's disapproval, and conflict with your partner?

I see it time and time again. The conflict may be complex but the seeds that give birth to the conflict is simple enough. Appreciation is the heart and soul of what solidifies a relationship. Knowing that there's another soul who's on your side, who will acknowledge all the blood, sweat, and tears that you are expending, makes the game of life a little more simple.

So think about how it may be true for you. Think about how the conflict in your relationship may be a smokescreen for something much larger. Relationships require cooperation, sacrifice, give and take. The lubricant that keeps your relationship engine running smoothly is acknowledgment, recognition, and your willingness to articulate your appreciation for your partner.

Let's look at appreciation from your point of view for a moment. How important is it to you for your partner to express their appreciation of you? How do you feel when you believe that your partner has not acknowledged you? Do those feelings get expressed to your partner or acted out? Have you ever let your partner know how important it is to feel appreciated by them?

Let's walk through this step by step. Make a list of those qualities you possess for which you deserve to be acknowledged by your partner. Perhaps it's the consideration you exhibit towards your partner. Or the way you act responsibly towards your partner. Maybe you feel especially proud of the fact that you keep your partner's favorite cookies in the cupboard at all times. Whatever those qualities are, make the list as long as possible.

Now, look closely at this list. Think about all the times one or more of those items has gone unnoticed. How did that make you feel? Take at least three of the items listed above and write down how it makes you feel to have each quality go unacknowledged.

PART FIVE: APPRECIATION

The next step is extremely important. It's important to develop an awareness of how your hurt feelings get expressed—in words or in deeds? One premise of making molehills out of mountains is that you need to express your hurt rather than act it out. Acting out your hurt only perpetuates conflict rather than resolving it.

What actions do you use to express your hurt? Do you use the silent treatment? Do you take a hiatus from the relationship? Do you burn your partner's dinner? Do you *forget* to take the garbage out? Do you throw a temper tantrum?

The Magical Elixir

The most important thing to remember is that when appreciation is withheld, there's invariably going to be hurt feelings. Whenever there are hurt feelings, the potential exists for conflict. Our goal is to better handle conflict by expressing our hurt rather than acting it out.

Your willingness to express your hurt is an important key to resolving the underlying relationship issues. Your willingness to express your appreciation for your partner will go a long way towards insuring that your partner will return the favor in kind. That is the ultimate formula for reducing the hurt and resentment that two people feel towards each other.

Beauty's in the Eye of the Beholder

Over the piano was printed a notice. Please do not shoot the pianist. He is doing his best.

-Oscar Wilde

PART FIVE: APPRECIATION

Bridge-Builder's Tip

As you sow the seeds of appreciation for your partner, you will begin to reap a harvest of love and kindness in return.

"Ray, Ray, here, up here, I'm in the office. Come on up, I want to show you something."

The excitement in Jill's voice told Ray that something was up. Jill had been acting mysterious all week, however she wouldn't say what was going on.

But today Jill had finally finished her secret project and now she was just waiting for Ray to come home. She couldn't wait to show him the story she had written, having worked on it for days while Ray was at work. Writing had been a long forgotten passion she had promised herself she was going to get back to someday. Someday had rolled around last week when she finally sat down at the computer.

Jill was surprised at how good it felt. That's what was so amazing about writing. The sense of pride that came with creating something from nothing. Unearthing new nuggets about herself from within. Shaping and molding those nuggets into cogent thoughts to be shared with the world. Impacting even one person's life, it gave her the chills just thinking about it.

But the best feeling of all was being able to share her work with Ray. He was going to be so proud of her. He

Beauty's in the Eye of the Beholder

was the one who was pushing her to start writing again. So, she couldn't wait for him to read the story. There was so much in the story about her that she wanted to share with Ray.

"Jill, what's up? What's all the commotion about?" Ray asked, huffing and puffing from running up the three flights of stairs.

Without saying a word, Jill handed Ray a folder that contained the twenty pages the story was written on. "I want you to read this."

"Don't tell me. You didn't! When did you do all of this? Jill, you finally... I can't believe it!"

Ray hugged Jill. He was so proud of her. He had wanted her to do this for so long.

"Go ahead. Sit down and read it. I just finished it an hour ago. I'm sure there are still some typos. Promise me you won't feel compelled to point those out to me."

"*Moi*. Never," he chuckled.

Ray had already begun reading the first page. There was a smile here, a grunt there. His forehead would furrow. Next, his face broke into a big smile. The next page brought complete silence, steadied concentration. Page after page, Jill watched intently, interpreting his every expression and sound.

Finally, ten minutes later, Ray put down the last sheet of paper. As he took his glasses off, Jill noticed for the first time, there were tears streaming down Ray's cheeks. Those tears said it all for Jill.

Effort. Sacrifice. Talent. Ability. Worth. Value. Who doesn't want to feel appreciated for what they do, for who they are? You recognize how good it feels when those longings for appreciation have been stroked.

PART FIVE: APPRECIATION

It doesn't matter how big or small the *project* is. It can be something grand like graduating from college or something seemingly trivial like cleaning out a closet.

It doesn't matter how big or small the *gesture* is. It can be something grand like throwing a surprise birthday party or something seemingly trivial like bringing your child's forgotten umbrella to school.

It doesn't matter how big or small the *acknowledgment* is. It can be something grand like a testimonial dinner thrown in your honor for the years of service you provided to your local community or something seemingly trivial like getting your dad an apron with the words *World's Best Chef* printed on it.

Feeling appreciated by the people in our lives is an incredible tonic. Having who we are and what we do acknowledged is a magical feeling. And I'm sure you recognize the devastation you feel when the craving to be acknowledged, to feel appreciated goes unmet. Criticism stings. Being ignored altogether devastates. Yet, all too often people stop taking the time to be kind to one another. The reasons may vary—indifference, being distracted, spite, too many demands and too little time.

Withholding your appreciation can feel like an act of betrayal to your partner. See it from their point of view. Giving so much of themselves, yet you remain blind to those efforts.

Of course there are times when things just get misunderstood. The excitement in your voice isn't enough. The inflection is flat. The words don't match your partner's expectations. Or you don't know what to do or say.

Whatever the reason, no matter the justification, whenever appreciation is held back, however it's held back, the pain becomes forever etched in our soul. We don't soon forget when that special investment in something near and dear to us goes unnoticed. We keep a list. We check it twice. And believe me, that list becomes the source of much of the turmoil and conflict if the hurt doesn't get expressed.

The good news is, things don't have to stay this way forever. What experience has taught me is that most people genuinely are appreciative of their partner. Most of us are able to recognize the uniqueness of our partner. Most people have a good perspective of their partner's qualities that lend so much to the well-being of their relationship.

No, the problem is not being able to recognize those qualities. The problem is the many misunderstandings that are created when we become angry at or disappointed in our partner's words and deeds. You see when that emotional energy takes over the relationship, a different kind of climate takes over that perpetuates ill-will rather than puts out the fire.

Once a climate of ill-will takes over, any feelings of appreciation go right out the window. Once you see your partner as your antagonist, it's impossible to keep the perspective that your partner is a valued friend. When you get to that place where you lose perspective about who your partner is, you need to find a way to balance out your feelings of hurt and betrayal with your other feelings of attraction and appreciation. Let me show you a couple of tools to reestablish equilibrium in order restore a climate of acceptance and appreciation.

PART FIVE: APPRECIATION

Bridge-Builder's Tool

Celebrate rather than evaluate your partner.

Mort was bursting with pride as he walked into my office. He couldn't wait for me to sit down so he could show me what he was holding in his hand.

"Steve, look what I got last night," Mort said.

"What do you have there?" I asked.

"It's a chip, my thirty day chip. I did it. I got it. I finally got it. Thirty days straight without using. Who da thunk it? Me going that long without a drink."

I looked at the chip and then returned it to Mort. "Hey how about that! Congratulations! How does it feel?"

"I can't tell you how good it was to finally get this. It has taken me six months to put together thirty straight days of clean time.

"Everyone was so happy for me at the meeting last night. That's what made it so special—the feedback they gave me."

"What do you mean?" I asked.

"No one dwelled on how long it took me to get my thirty day chip. I was scared to go to the meeting last night because I thought I would have to replay every mistake I've made over the last six months. I thought for sure that everyone would offer some remembrance of how I had messed up over and over again."

"I'm guessing that it didn't happen that way," I offered.

"No, it was the strangest thing. People congratulated me. But they also told me how much my coming to the meetings every week for the last six months meant to them. Some people said that knowing me made a difference in their lives. Can you believe it? Me making a difference in somebody else's life? Now there's a switch!

"I felt as if they were telling me that I mattered to them. No one ever tells me that. All I ever hear is how I screwed up, but these people actually made me feel as if I'm all right no matter what I do or how I do it."

Celebrating rather than evaluating a person. Affirming who they are rather than focusing on how well they do something. You tell me, what feels better to you, being affirmed or being evaluated?

Do you see the shift that might be made? Let go of all the hurtful ways you evaluate your partner. Don't confuse who a person is with the actions that person takes. You know the saying, "Hate the sin, love the sinner." That means you need to surrender the need to make you partner out to be good or bad, right or wrong, your way or no way.

Are you ready to make such a shift in your relationship? Are you ready to celebrate the uniqueness of who your partner is? Your partner is going through life the best way they know how. Evaluating that process merely conveys your judgments. Being able to celebrate how that process enables your partner to express the essence of who they are enables your partner to feel appreciated by you.

PART FIVE: APPRECIATION

Bridge-Builder's Tool

Create an energy of gratitude rather than disappointment towards your partner.

"I could never see it before," Mark said.

"See what?" I asked

"See what you meant, see how I burdened Shirley with how deprived I felt, how I was always disappointed in her. I just couldn't look at it any other way. I felt like I wasn't getting what I wanted. I wanted more of her, her attention, her love, her time.

"The more I felt deprived, the more let down I felt, the more I demanded what I wasn't getting. I didn't see the damage it was doing to our relationship," Mark sighed.

"What did you finally realize?" I asked.

"I finally saw how I was sabotaging Shirley. All I could focus on were the things that our relationship wasn't. I never stopped to think how dumping all that energy on Shirley actually made it harder for her to be there for me.

"I saw how she was constantly backpedaling from me. I thought she was punishing me, but I finally realized she was just trying to protect herself.

"Of course by then, she was so angry at me, she felt like everything she did was wrong, there was no way she was going to reach out to me," Mark said, shaking his head at the sheer futility of it all.

"Hindsight is twenty-twenty," I said.

"Yea, that's when I finally decided to try what you suggested. So I sat down and made a list of things that I was grateful for, you know all the wonderful things that Shirley was, all the things I had because of our relationship. The funny thing was, I didn't have to think hard about that at all. I didn't realize how much I had to feel grateful about.

"So after making the list, every day for the next three weeks, I thanked Shirley each night for bringing to my life one of the items from my list."

"How did that work out for you?" I asked.

"I gotta tell you, it was hard at first. I felt funny doing it. I would do the exercise every night before we went to bed. But I felt so self-conscious. You know, I couldn't talk to her without turning out the lights first," Mark said with a sheepish grin on his face.

"That's okay. Did it help?" I asked.

"A little. It still was awkward. And Shirley didn't really trust me at first. She thought I was trying to trick her, I guess.

"But you know what? The funniest thing was that the more I expressed my gratitude, little by little, I didn't feel so disappointed in her anymore.

"I mean, it was weird. Shirley started paying more attention to me. She would do things with me, for me, without me asking. Before, it seemed like if I asked, that was the one way to insure that things would never happen."

"So the moral of the story is?" I asked.

"By expressing gratitude for the fruits of what my relationship bears, I can fill some of the holes that my relationship needs filling."

Do you understand what is being suggested? There are

PART FIVE: APPRECIATION

two feelings that impede your willingness to create an energy of appreciation and gratitude in your relationship. Entitlement and disappointment. When you live with the mindset that you're entitled to what you want when you want it, the only possible outcome of such an attitude is feeling disappointed and deprived.

When those two feelings begin to consume you, you likely dump those feelings upon your partner. Then you devise all kinds of schemes to get what you want from your partner.

Think of those feelings—entitlement, feeling let down, disappointed, resentful. Do you realize that all those feelings that you experience and express are energy? How does being consumed with that energy affect you? How does expressing that energy to your partner affect them?

When you make demands upon your partner that they are either unwilling or incapable of meeting, how does the energy from the resultant tug of war color your relationship? Can you see how the energy can transform your relationship into a war zone? And, I hope you realize by now, if the underlying issue—how unappreciated you or your partner are feeling—goes unnoticed, then the war will most likely continue.

So let me suggest a shift for you. This shift will completely change the energy that flows between you and your partner. By making this shift, you can expect three things to change immediately. First, your partner will feel appreciated by you rather than condemned by you. Second, your partner will feel more open to addressing your concerns. Third, your energy will shift, leaving you feeling more fulfilled and less disappointed.

The shift goes something like this: transform your feelings of hurt, resentment, and disappointment by expressing appreciation for who your partner is and what it is they give to you.

Let me walk you through this. First, make a list of what it is you're feeling disappointed about with your partner. Write down how this sense of disappointment makes you feel.

PART FIVE: APPRECIATION

Now, write down the things that you appreciate about your partner and the things that your relationship does give to you.

Third, create a plan with your partner to discuss the items on your list. I suggest that you do this slowly, perhaps discussing only one item per day.

_____
_____
_____
_____
_____
_____
_____
_____
_____
_____
_____
_____
_____
_____
_____
_____
_____
_____

Patience is the key ingredient for this skill to be effective. Feeling unappreciated leaves long lasting scars. Healing comes with time and consistency as you and your partner begin to trust the genuineness of what each of you is expressing. But rest assured, you can bring healing to the wounds that exist between you and your partner if you're willing to use the simple tools we talked about in this chapter.

PART 6
Power and Control

*It's not whether you win or lose but how
you play the game.*

-Thomas Matthews

What's All the Fighting About?

The feeling we have that we deserve to have everything just the way we want it ends up destroying spontaneity.

-Linda Weltner

PART SIX: POWER AND CONTROL

"I don't need no shrink to tell me what the problem is. I understand only too well. What she needs is a good hobby or even to go back to work."

"The problem is your wife isn't busy enough?" I asked, trying to understand his read on the situation.

"That's all it boils down to. She just has too much time on her hands. When she starts to thinking, she starts making herself unhappy."

"Your wife's unhappy because she thinks unhappy thoughts?" I asked.

"Well, now you're making it too simplified. I know that it's more than that. But, honestly, Doc, what's all this mumbo jumbo about 'my needs, my needs?'"

"Your wife's needs are mumbo jumbo?" I asked.

"Now Doc, come on, don't go making me out to be the bad guy here. You're starting to confuse me. What I mean to say is, what's so all fire important about her needs? You never hear me complaining about my emotional needs do you?"

"You question the importance of what your wife wants from you?" I asked.

"You know, Doc, why is it that when you say it, I feel like such a heel? Of course what she wants from me is important, I guess. It's just that, well, you don't know how my wife is. You gotta be firm with her. You can't give in. You gotta hold the line."

"Your marriage is a competitive game like football, where you have to have a strategy for everything?" I asked.

"Now, Doc, I swear you're putting words into my

mouth. I didn't say any such thing. It's just that, if you give her an inch, she'll take a mile. You know what I mean?"

"I'm afraid I don't," I replied.

"Well, listen then. I know exactly what will happen. It starts out with wanting to be hugged. Everytime I see her, she gets this funny look in her eyes. And I know there ain't no just doing it *once*.

"It doesn't start and end with just one hug. Then she wants me to start kissing her when I come home at night. Can't you see what I'm getting at?"

"You don't know how to say 'no' once you say 'yes?'" I guessed.

"Well no, that's not what I mean at all. What I mean is, if it was just the hugging and the kissing, I could put up with that, I suppose. But you know where this all is heading, don't you?"

"I must admit, you're ahead of me on this, why don't you tell me," I replied.

"Look. I could put up with the occasional peck on the cheek. The hug, well, we all have to make compromises. But then the thing that comes next, the thing I hate worse than anything.

"Next, she'll want us to start having talks. Like going for a walk or sitting on the patio after dinner.

"No way. No how. Not in this lifetime.

"I mean I've got a life too, you know. That's what I'm saying to you, Doc. If you don't draw the line in the beginning, she'll just keep taking and taking and taking. And what happens to me in all of this?

"How will I have time for myself? How will I be able to do the things I want to do, if we start paying so much attention to what she wants all the time?

PART SIX: POWER AND CONTROL

"Why can't she be like me? I ask very little of the world. Hey, life's tough, but you just gotta learn to be there for yourself. There's no sense counting on anybody else."

"You would like it if she just held her breath?" I asked.

"Now, there you go again. You didn't hear me say that, did you? It's just, why doesn't she learn to tough things out? That's what works best for me."

I looked at him with a hint of resignation in my eyes and said, "I don't know. Your solution to just say no seems to me to be a prescription for disaster rather than a means to be involved with your partner."

Is my friend in the story merely selfish, self-centered, insensitive, and uncaring? Perhaps so, but what value is there in thinking of him that way? If we relate to him only on that basis, we have guaranteed ourselves a neverending struggle based on name calling and justifying one's behavior.

No, I prefer to think of my friend as merely frightened. Maybe he could express that more clearly, but I think it's undeniable that beneath all of his insensitivities beats the heart of somebody who's terrified of what will happen to him anytime he gives in to his wife.

It's clear that he sees the only way to take care of himself is to dig his heels in, to withhold what his wife wants from him. It's easy to see the inevitable disaster that comes when the ways he protects himself denies his partner at the same time.

But this is the issue over which much of the conflict is waged in our relationships. *Power and control.* Two of the dirtiest words in any relationship. "You're so controlling." "All he wants is to be in control." It's like waving a red cape in front of a bull. Bring on power and control and *let the games begin.*

Power and control. *Them are fighting words.* Power and control. These two words can take any aspect of a relationship and escalate conflict to its highest pitched frenzy. Power and control. These energies hide so much of what's buried beneath the surface of any relationship.

But have you stopped to think about this? Have you stopped to think about the fact that controlling behavior serves to mask something deeper within? Can you see how controlling behavior masks your fears? Does it make sense to you that the vortex created by the battles waged over power and control are merely the means to bury the fears that live beneath the surface of any relationship?

Our fears are many. We need some manner to quell them. Think about my friend in the previous story. Think about what he may be so frightened of. Can you see how frightened he is to allow himself to get close to his wife? Just imagine how frightening it is for him to have someone be vulnerable with him. Do you get the sense that he believes that the only way to insure his autonomy is by resisting? Can you see how his sense of independence becomes threatened by the mere suggestion that he go along with what his wife would like him to do?

If you listen hard enough, it's easy to hear how overwhelmed he is by his own needs and vulnerabilities. And so he needs a way to disconnect from what he's feeling. He needs a way to turn down the intensity. He needs a way to insure that he doesn't have to experience what frightens him so much. Bring on the control—turn up the power.

It saddens me when I watch him stir up chaos in order to deny his own humanness. That's what he's really denying. His emotional needs, he being the sustenance for his wife's needs, his desire to protect his autonomy, his fear

PART SIX: POWER AND CONTROL

of not being able to influence his life, these are all part of being human. However, these aspects of being human—depending upon somebody else, needing somebody else, working cooperatively with somebody else—are all too often viewed as being an expression of being weak, insecure, and fragile.

So my friend goes through life cut off from much of his humanity. He suffers for it. His partner suffers for it. Ultimately, his relationship suffers for it, as well.

That's what much of what the drama is about. The endless tug-of-wars. The pushing, the pulling. Digging your heels in. Defiance. Entrenched positions. Inflexibility.

What's going on beneath the surface? What self-protective mode are we in when we find ourselves part of an endless arm wrestling match with our partner?

Wanting things our way. Trying to hold on to what we have. Believing the only way to keep what we've got is to never let go. Frightened that if we do let go, we'll suffer forever.

Wanting to have a say in our destiny. Always having to believe we can influence the uninfluenceable. Without question, the drama is important to understand for what it expresses about what's going on beneath the surface.

There's much churning beneath the struggle, beneath the need to control, beneath the need to distance ourselves from our sense of vulnerability. In the next two chapters we'll examine more closely two crucial issues that are the underbelly of much of the surface behaviors associated with power and control. These two issues are the fears provoked by emotional intimacy and the fears provoked by our loss of autonomy as we begin to blend our lives with another person.

Make Up to Break Up

Love is letting go of fear.

-Gerald Jampolsky

PART SIX: POWER AND CONTROL

Bridge-Builder's Tip

*Love, patience, and kindness soothe the fear
that sabotages your relationships.*

Today, she's my very best friend in the whole wide world. But it didn't just happen—no indeed, we both have the emotional scars to prove that. Anyway, we were getting together for the first time in a couple of years. The funny thing was, it seemed as if it had only been a couple of weeks rather than years.

That's the way it had always been for Carly and me. Carly was part of the gang in high school, but to me, she was more than just a friend. We've always made it a point to do more than just check in from time to time. We make time to be with each other, to reconnect, most importantly to celebrate what our lives have become.

Although today we care very deeply about each other, it wasn't always easy for Carly and me. That took time, patience, and an awful lot of understanding. As we were talking on the ride home from the airport, I couldn't help but think back to the old days when our friendship was more like pulling teeth than anything else.

Things didn't just fall into place all at once for us. We didn't always get it, get what came between us, get what made it hard for her to let me be her friend. No, that understanding came with a lot of tears, a lot of anger, and sadly a lot of time spent apart.

Thankfully, after awhile, the pieces did begin to fit. But initially, I had no understanding of her, her fears, no understanding of how my wanting to be her friend activated those fears. Looking back, it's easy to see how so much of what went on between us in those early years was her testing me every way she could think of. But back then, all I could understand was there was always drama, conflict; there was always us coming together and pulling apart.

In those days it was open season, everything was tested—the genuineness of my feelings, the loyalty I felt towards her. She tested me by seeing just how unlovable she could make herself, waiting and watching, checking out my reaction. Would I stay or would I go?

Now, don't get me wrong. In the beginning, I flunked more of those tests than I passed. But once I caught on, I was better able to *understand* her fears rather than *react* to her behavior. I began to see how fragile she could become. This enabled me to stop judging how she behaved. Finally, I began to understand how her *expressed* feelings and actions were tools of self-protection rather than weapons of mass destruction. Gratefully, I began to see the choices I could exercise—react or respond, personalize her actions and expressed feelings or put them in their appropriate context.

Eventually, disengaging from Carly's behavior became a little easier for me to do. I began to play this game in my mind—was the conflict we were having *me-based* or *fear-based*. If the argument was *me-based*, I knew there was some action I could take to shift my behavior. If the

PART SIX: POWER AND CONTROL

argument was *fear-based*, I knew I needed to be patient and accepting of where Carly was at emotionally.

The more I was able to disengage from the swirl of chaos, the better able I could see what her fears were. One thing was very clear to me—Carly was absolutely unwilling to build a friendship with me based upon me meeting her emotional needs.

That may sound odd. Why wouldn't someone want another person to be there for them, to care about them? Why would it be so painful for Carly to let me in? Why would she turn the offer of my unconditional love into a raging battlefield?

Little by little I learned that she had good reasons for doing so. The details of her life aren't as important as the impact those details had on her willingness to create a close relationship with me.

For her, it just made more sense to put her efforts into pushing me away, discouraging my efforts at trying to get close, pulling the plug on our connection when it became too intense. I came to accept that she wasn't rejecting me, she was protecting herself. She was protecting herself from being vulnerable. She was protecting herself from being hurt one more time. Carly was only making her world a safe place for *her* to be.

You see, my efforts at wanting to befriend her merely activated many of the fears she had about human friendship. And at the core of those fears, were her fears about needing another human being. To make a long story short, the early lessons she learned about how safe it was to need another person would move any of us to protect ourselves rather than invite someone into our world.

The shame she felt when she would look to her

parents for love and acceptance only to receive ridicule or anger or even worse than that—indifference.

The confusion she would feel everytime she asked for help, only to be made to feel like she was a burden.

The fear she would feel everytime she saw her mother ridiculed by her father for being human.

The terror that would fill her body every time she saw her father explode at her mother for being *too demanding*.

The trepidation she would feel at not knowing whether her mother was in her gentle persona or if she had arisen in her *terminator* persona on any particular day.

The self-doubt and inadequacy that would fill her when she couldn't come up with an explanation other than *she just wasn't worth* taking the time to be parented, to be guided, to be directed in her life.

No, these were not the lessons that would make anybody conclude that needing another person was a rewarding experience. There was no basis for her to feel safe entrusting anybody with the vulnerable parts of who she was.

And so she did what any of us would do. She controlled. She fought. She pushed away. She tested. She stomped. She kicked. She screamed. She tried to run the show all by herself. Carly would do battle with anybody who dared to get close. She would come and go, but mostly just go.

At the time we initially crossed paths, we did battle more often than not. But as time moved on, we were able to find a different emotional space other than her fear, mistrust, and emotional unavailability to build a relationship that we will both value till the day we die.

From the surface, it looks familiar. Two people trapped in a dance of chaos. The cause is seemingly noble—wanting to connect, to be close. But invariably, all efforts fall short. Their words say that they want to connect. But their behavior reveals a much more fundamental truth about what's bubbling beneath the surface. Fear. Trepidation. Uncertainty. Ambivalence.

And so it is that the diversionary tactics begin. The arguments. The times spent apart. The coming together. The pledges that we'll never be this stupid again. But a day later, a week later, a month later, it's back in your face again. The same patterns, the same methods of avoidance, the same hurt and sorrow.

For how many of you is this true? How many of you feel like you get swallowed up in a cycle of non-specific fears, undeniable dread, explanations of why you should go your separate ways, explanations you barely believe yourself? For how many of you is the appearance of this dread and discomfort the precursor to arguments, chaos, separating and coming back together again? For how many of you does the uncomfortable feelings, the resultant chaos to distract you from those feelings send you into survival mode?

Do you know what I mean by survival mode? The behaviors may vary but the goal is always the same—to be in control. It may be as obvious as breaking up with your partner or taking a *hiatus* from the relationship. It could be more subtle such as giving your partner the silent treatment. Whatever the means, whatever the style, the goal is undeniably the same—to control access, to limit one's ability to reach you, to lessen the demands for emotional intimacy that you fear are being placed upon you.

Let's be clear. The need to protect yourself is your highest calling. No person, no thing will ever be placed above that need. Let's also be clear that many battles are needlessly waged in the name of self-protection.

Why are these battles needlessly waged? I hope the answer to that question is obvious to you by now. Because you stay focused on the circumstances without talking about the underlying relationship issue.

Can you see how many of the fears you have about needing another person get transformed into the conflicts you *create* to keep that very person away? Can you see how the inevitable fears we all have about emotional intimacy get masked by the chaos and conflicts that divert our attention from expressing those underlying fears.

No, it's much safer to moralize about our partner's controlling behavior than it is to have an honest discussion about the fears that get activated when two people get close to one another. It's much safer to invest our emotional and intellectual energy into creating solutions to the diversionary conflict we create, than building bridges that are based upon our emotional needs and vulnerabilities.

The chaos we create on the surface masks the struggle waged beneath the surface. We can call our partner names. We can label them as controlling or power hungry. The choice is always there to get sucked into the struggle. You can always escalate the battle with your own assertion of control and power.

But that's not a solution, it's a reaction. We all kid ourselves that a reaction will get us what we want. You know the truth by now. In order to get what you want, you have to hitch your wagon to a horse other than the one we call *control*.

The horse I'm referring to has been talked about

throughout this book in various forms. Acceptance. Understanding. Patience. Kindness. Secure connections. Emotional safety. You have to dive beneath the chaos. Dig underneath the power struggles. Look within your partner for what they are so afraid of. Examine within yourself how well your demanding ways work.

It takes two people to create a power struggle. It takes only one person to act in a kind, understanding fashion towards somebody else. You see, it really is as simple as what you choose to do with what appears in your life.

Let's get practical for a moment. I've tried to illuminate for you throughout this book the necessary shifts that would be helpful for you to make. Any shift you make is always predicated upon one thing—being able to identify the options you have.

It's no different here. You have the option of seeing much of your conflict as based upon power and control or based on somebody's fears that are provoked when they get close to another person.

Let's first examine some of the vulnerabilities you may feel as you get close to another person. Perhaps it's discomfort with needing somebody, or fear that you'll be abandoned if you let someone into your life. Maybe you feel uncomfortable having to be accountable to another person. Whatever your fears are, take some time and write down what they are.

The next step is becoming more aware of how these fears appear in your relationship. They may be as obvious as breaking off the relationship. You may provoke arguments with your partner to shift the focus away from what you're feeling. You may experience yourself not being as connected to your partner. You may call less frequently. You may limit how long you talk on the phone. You may start screening your calls. Whatever it is you do, let's see if there's a connection between how you begin to control the relationship and the fears you have about getting close to your partner.

PART SIX: POWER AND CONTROL

The last step should be obvious by now. You need to begin talking to your partner about your fears and how your fears appear in your relationship. The reason is simple. Talking about these issues lessens the power they hold on you. When you take ownership of your fears and the way those fears appear in your relationship, you'll be able to work with your partner rather than against your partner.

At the same time, take things slow. My ol' prescription of one part patience and one part kindness applies here more so than anywhere else. This is big stuff that doesn't go away with one exercise in a book. It goes away over time when love and kindness replace fear and the many different ways we mask our fears.

Simply keep in mind that wherever there's behavior that you experience as controlling, there's fear right below the surface. You have a choice to respond to the controlling behavior or the array of emotions beneath the surface. I hope you learn to respond to what's going on beneath the surface. I'll settle for the time when you do a little of each rather than merely reacting to the behavior on the surface.

Take It to the Limit One More Time

Love creates an 'us' without destroying a 'me.'

-Leo Buscaglia

PART SIX: POWER AND CONTROL

Bridge-Builder's Tip

Honoring your partner rather than fighting for your self-interests will lessen the conflict in your relationship.

"I want to join this club, but I don't know. There's so much they expect from you."

"Like what?" I asked.

"First off, they have this meeting you have to attend. It's the third Thursday of every month. I'm not going to give up my Thursday night just like that."

"It sounds like it's important for you to have a say in how, when, and where you spend your time," I observed.

"Well, yea, of course it is. What if I want to do something the week they have their meeting? I should have the choice of whether I attend their meeting, shouldn't I?"

"You feel like you're giving up a lot by joining this club?" I asked.

"Well, yea, of course I do. And I haven't told you the half of it. There's more to it. They expect you to join a committee to head a yearly volunteer project."

"That disturbs you?" I asked.

"Well, yea. Why are there so many conditions? Look, I'm paying dues to join this club. Isn't that enough? What are all of these hoops that I have to jump through just to become a member of their club?"

"It sure sounds like you believe you have to give up a

lot to join. What's so great about being a member in the first place?"

"I told you all about that before. It will be great for my career. I'll be able to meet a lot of people who can help me out. You know, you can't get anywhere in this field without somebody who will take an interest in your career. And this is where all the *main players* hang out.

"Besides that, it can't hurt my social life any. There are functions that go on throughout the year. And some of them are pretty impressive to attend."

"Well, it sounds like there's a lot for you to gain by joining. Why's it so hard for you?"

"I just don't like being told what to do and when to do it. I feel like somebody else is controlling my life. And if this is what you have to do just to join, then what's it going to be like a year from now?

"First, they're taking away my Thursday nights. Then they want to assign me to a committee to work with a bunch of people I don't even know. Then, they have this whole list of rules about how you have to act if you're a member of their club.

"It just seems to me that I should be able to have some say in all of this."

"Well, it sounds like a real dilemma. On the one hand, you stand to gain a lot of visibility for your career. You'll have the opportunity to rub elbows with important people who can support your development. You've been complaining lately about how bored you are with your social life. This sounds like just the shot in the arm you were hoping for. You'll even have the opportunity to do some good work for the community.

"On the other hand, you're digging your heels in

because you don't like other people telling you what to do. You're fearful of how much control this club will exert over your life. You feel like your ability to make decisions is being curtailed. You resent having to do things somebody else's way. Most importantly, you don't want to surrender in any way to somebody else."

"Yea, that's right!"

"I can understand how this decision is so hard for you."

The struggle my friend is experiencing is not unique to him. Relationships challenge us to master the delicate balancing act of maintaining and surrendering parts of our individuality. The art of building relationship-bridges challenges us to cooperatively blend two separate lives into a singular entity that honors the needs of each individual, yet preserves the integrity and well-being of the relationship.

Don't get me wrong. I assure you that last sentence was much easier for me to write than it is for any of us to execute. However, it's the secret to the ongoing work we take on in our relationships.

There's no question that the road gets rocky from time to time. And I'm sure that you can see by now, that when the road gets rocky, there's something important going on beneath the surface of the relationship that isn't getting expressed. However, how many of you focus more on the drama created by the power struggle rather than what the power struggle is masking about the underlying relationship issues? For instance...

While you get caught up in *defending the correctness* of your position, do you lose sight of what the drama is expressing about you and your partner and the emotional needs of both?

While you get caught up in creating a space in your relationship that *protects your individuality,* do you compromise the well-being of your relationship?

While you get caught up in *enforcing your position,* do you totally disconnect from what your underlying fears are?

While you get caught up in *justifying the righteousness* of your cause, do you turn your back on the dignity of your partner?

Power and control is fear driven. The more you want to disconnect from feeling your fear, the more you will mask your fear with controlling behavior. One of the many fears that lives beneath all the drama that power and control creates is the fear of losing our autonomy. For instance, think about this conversation I overheard one night while I was visiting my friend Sylvia at her bar.

I was nursing a Miller as I munched on a bowl of mixed nuts. Sylvia was in the midst of some animated conversation with one of the patrons at the bar. I had one eye on the Bulls game on the big screen TV, but what had really caught my attention was the conversation going on at the table next to me between two gentlemen.

"Then she said, 'I would appreciate it very much if you would trim your mustache. It tickles me when you kiss me.'"

"I told her I wouldn't do it. That I would trim my mustache when I was ready to trim my mustache, not when she tells me to. When she asked me why I wouldn't do it, I simply told her, 'Because I can't have you believe I'm going to do something for you everytime you ask me to. I need you to know that when I do something it's because that's what I want to do.'"

His friend nodded his head as he said, "I know what

PART SIX: POWER AND CONTROL

you mean. I just went through something similar the other night with Laurie."

He continued, "Laurie had been staying away from me lately. All we seemed to do was argue about how much time we were going to spend together. Well, I figured if she was going to be that way, I would fix her. I knew she called me every night at 9:00 p.m. sharp, so, when she called me one night, I let the answering machine pick up the phone.

"She spent the next three hours trying to get ahold of me but I wouldn't answer the phone.

"The next day when we did talk to each other, she asked me where I was last night. I told her I decided to go out to a couple of bars. Let me tell you, she was out of her mind with jealousy. She became enraged. She asked me how I could do that to her. Her exact words were 'How do you expect me to trust you if you're going to act like this?'"

The man finished his story by telling his friend, "Of course, I showed her. I told her that I didn't care whether she ever trusted me or not. That seemed to solve it right there!"

Trimming mustaches. Going to bars. Is that the root of what's going in these guys' relationships? Or is it more likely that there's some struggle taking place between them and their partners that they haven't even begun to talk about? Is it more likely that the power struggles that they've created mask the fears that they have about trying to cooperatively solve the problems in their relationships?

Can you guess what they're frightened of? Frightened that they won't get their way? Frightened that they won't get what they want when they want it? Frightened that they'll lose some essential part of who they are if they give into their partner's *demands*? Frightened that if they give in one time, they'll lose and their partner will win? Frightened if they give in just this one time, they'll always have to give in?

These are many of the fears that bubble beneath the surface when two people try to blend their lives. It's only natural to want to cling to our sense of autonomy, our own way of doing things. Yet, it's this very natural desire to want to hold on to who we are, how we do what we do, that becomes the precipitant for so much of what gets fought over without ever being acknowledged.

There's no question that the fears need to be honored. They can't be wished away, talked away, or even threatened away. The best any of us can do is acknowledge that the fears are present. If you can acknowledge to yourself and to your partner what you're so frightened of, then you can begin to support rather than fight with each other.

You see, that's the only way you can defuse the situation. Supporting each other. Support means compromise. Support means shifting priorities. Support means balancing the relationship's needs against the individual needs of each person. Support means being there for each other rather than competing with each other.

That's the biggest shift that needs to be made. Shifting from seeing your interests as competing to creating shared interests that support the well-being of the relationship. That's the ultimate art of blending your life with your partner. Creating an environment of cooperation rather than competition.

So let's take a look at your relationships. Let's see what shifts need to be made to make your relationship less

PART SIX: POWER AND CONTROL

competitive and more cooperative. More importantly, let's see if we can discover what your fears are that create the power struggles that exist in your relationship.

First, identify some power struggles that you experience with your partner. It could be as silly as the infamous toilet seat battle. It could be as important as the politics that revolve around your sexual life. It could be as boring as who cleans the dishes. It could be as fundamental as who controls the money. I'm sure you can think of at least three points of conflict where power and control keep you and your partner paralyzed in winning and losing rather than emancipated by the spirit of resolution.

___

Next, look more closely at each example you wrote above. Answer this only from *your* perspective. What's the fear that's buried under the power struggle? Why do you cling so hard to your position? What are you afraid will happen to you if you let go of your position and create a solution of compromise?

_____
_____
_____
_____
_____
_____
_____
_____
_____
_____
_____
_____
_____
_____
_____
_____
_____
_____
_____
_____

Now, the hard part. One by one, examine each example. Examine the fears that you associate with each example. What's a compromise that incorporates your partner's interests with your interests? Take your time. Thoughtfully consider what a favorable solution is for all three concerns—you, your partner, and the relationship.

PART SIX: POWER AND CONTROL

This is hard to do but it's where you're going to eventually wind up if you want to move beyond the power struggle. Ask yourself, just how much more do you want to invest in the power struggle? Have you invested enough or do you want to keep it going? If you're ready to be through with it, here's the path out of the struggle.

The key point to remember when we're talking about power and control is that you're really dealing with fear. Fear is something that you need to respect. When you respect the underlying fears below the surface, you're much more able to work with the fears rather than untangle the knots of the power struggle that's raging above the surface.

That's it for the themes of the four underlying relationship issues. Rest assured that they won't always appear as obvious as they sound in this book. But as you become more sensitized to what these four themes are and how they appear in your relationships, you'll begin to feel more comfortable with how best to resolve the underlying relationship issues.

Recognizing the themes is one half of the battle. Resolving the issues once you recognize the theme is the second half of the battle. To more effectively resolve these issues, you're going to need a blueprint and some tools to execute the plan. Join me in the next section to learn how to do just that.

PART 7
Making Molehills Out of Mountains

The only way to even approach doing something perfectly is through experience, and experience is the name everyone gives to their mistakes.

-Oscar Wilde

The Blueprint for Resolution

For the things we have to learn before we can do them,
we learn by doing them.

-Aristotle

PART SEVEN: MAKING MOLEHILLS OUT OF MOUNTAINS

Let's move forward by first reviewing where we've been. Making molehills out of mountains is a process of conflict resolution that enables you to forge understanding, resolution, and forgiveness out of the disagreements and unresolved conflict that exist between you and your partner.

The mechanism that enables you to create such a transformation is a relationship skill I've called *pinpointing the issue*. Remember, the first premise of pinpointing the issue is that there are *two* levels to most unresolved conflict—the *circumstance* and the *underlying relationship issue*. The circumstance is the event that *precipitates* the conflict between you and your partner. The underlying relationship issue is the *unacknowledged* issue embedded in the circumstance of the conflict. I have discussed with you the four likeliest themes that the underlying issues might be: 1) feeling unaccepted; 2) unmet emotional needs; 3) feeling unappreciated; 4) power and control.

The second premise of pinpointing the issue is that many times two people choose to focus *only* on the first level of the conflict by trying to fix *only* the circumstances of a disagreement without acknowledging the underlying relationship issue. When this happens, it's inevitable that the circumstances of the conflict will continue to reappear until the presence of the underlying relationship issue is acknowledged and resolved.

The third premise of pinpointing the issue is that you have a *choice* as to how you'll address any existing conflict—fixing *only* the circumstances or fixing *both* the circumstances and resolving the underlying relationship issues. The advantage of addressing both the circumstance and the underlying relationship issue? By resolving the underlying relationship issue, you'll likely eliminate the need for the circumstances of the conflict to reappear in your relationship.

The fourth premise of pinpointing the issue is that there are signs and symptoms, think of them as cues, that an underlying unresolved relationship issue is present in your conflict. Let me take the time to identify for you what some of those cues are.

The first cue is what I refer to as being *stuck in the circle*. Being stuck in the circle is a familiar experience for most of us. Can you think of those times when the same disagreement appears over and over again? The disagreement doesn't go away no matter how much you try to make it go away. It's like a piece of toilet paper stuck to the bottom of your shoe. You can't seem to shake it no matter how hard you try.

When you begin to notice that you're revisiting an issue time and time again, it's likely that you're *stuck in the circle*. You may be noticing that all of your attempts at fixing the problem aren't working. If this is true for you, perhaps it's time to consider that there's an underlying unresolved relationship issue to address as well.

A second cue that might indicate the presence of an underlying relationship issue embedded in the circumstances of your conflict is if your reaction to what precipitated an argument is *out of proportion* to what actually precipitated the argument.

Here's how a friend of mine notices this cue when he runs into it with his wife. "Steve, I can tell that there's more to a disagreement than just the disagreement itself,

PART SEVEN: MAKING MOLEHILLS OUT OF MOUNTAINS

when on a scale of one to ten, the event we're squabbling about is a *two* but my reaction to that event is a *twelve*. That's when I know it's time for me to step back and figure out just what the hell else I need to be working out with my wife."

Here's an example of what I mean. Perhaps you and your partner come home one night and discover that your dog has tipped over the garbage can. While you begin to clean up the mess, your partner blames you for your dog's actions. Not only are you blamed for your dog's actions, but a whole list of grievances that date back to the first time the two of you met comes spilling out of your now agitated partner's mouth. When this happens, it's a good sign that there's much more going on than who's responsible for what an unattended dog does around the house.

One of my favorite cues that tells me I need to focus on an underlying relationship issue is when I begin to realize that I'm *keeping score* with somebody. You know, I'm keeping track of all the unfair things that are being done to me by somebody else. Or I make note of every mean thing said to me. There are times that I keep track of every inconsistent behavior that a person acts out. You know, those times when they do the very things to me that upsets them when I do it to them.

Scorekeeping is a sure sign that somebody's feeling unappreciated, that they're somehow feeling as if they're being treated unfairly. Unfortunately, taking ownership of those feelings often gets lost in all the work it takes to keep track of every perceived wrong that has been perpetrated.

You see, that's one of the problems with scorekeeping. You wind up putting more effort into documenting your emotional injuries than you do talking about your hurt feelings with your partner. It's a wonderful way to build a case against your partner, but how helpful is it as far as resolving anything? No, if you're putting more energy into tracking how unfair your partner is treating you, you're perpetuating conflict rather than resolving it.

Now, those are the four premises of pinpointing the issue. Don't lose sight of what mastering this principle will do for you. You'll lessen the burden that any relationship bears when there are unresolved relationship issues lurking in the background.

Snide remarks. Slippery evasions. Icy withdrawal. Cool indifference. Biting sarcasm. Stubbornness. These are the slings and arrows we cast when we weigh down our relationships with the emotional baggage derived from our unwillingness to resolve the issues in our relationships. The longer we give life to these issues, the greater toll they take on our emotional and spiritual well-being.

So, give yourself the opportunity to grow into the skills I have suggested throughout the book. Give yourself permission to wrestle with them. Some will feel more comfortable than others. You'll likely feel awkward with many of the shifts I've suggested. You don't have to use them all at once, or any of them at all for that matter.

Nothing is etched in stone. I've merely suggested ways to enhance your ability to lessen the conflict that exists in your relationship. Your job is to adapt those suggestions to your style. In creating your own style, you'll create a way of pinpointing the issue that suits you best.

Once you've pinpointed the issue, what do you do next? Here are some specific guidelines to follow as you begin to talk through the identified relationship issues.

PART SEVEN: MAKING MOLEHILLS OUT OF MOUNTAINS

Bridge-Builder's Tip

*Resolve your issues in a climate
of cooperation, not anger.*

Get your marker back out. I want you to underline this message. If you don't understand it, if you don't follow it, if the spirit of what I'm suggesting isn't honored, all of your hard work will go for naught. Pinpointing the issue *cannot* be performed in a climate of anger. Let me repeat that—pinpointing the issue *cannot* be done in a climate of anger. Resolving your underlying relationship issues must be done in a climate of *cooperation*.

Be clear about what I'm telling you. I'm not saying that you can't be, don't deserve to be, aren't entitled to be, angry, hurt, enraged, resentful or any combination of emotions. I'm simply saying that when you get down to the basics of pinpointing the issue, it must be done in a spirit of cooperation, not retaliation.

That makes sense, doesn't it? *Anger* is the energy by which you make a mountain out of a molehill. *Cooperation* is the energy by which you make a molehill out of a mountain.

So, what's the practical application to this? *Don't* attempt to resolve anything in the heat of the moment. If you or your partner are feeling too angry to constructively explore the relationship issues, don't do it at that point. It's okay to walk away until a time exists when cooler heads can prevail.

You can see why it's important to do this work in a

The Blueprint for Resolution

calmer climate, can't you? There's much for you to think about. There's much you need to understand beyond the pain that oozes from the wounds inflicted by your partner. More importantly, you need to see beyond your wounds long enough to see your partner's side of the disagreement, as well. All of this can only be done when you've had the time to defuse your emotions.

So it's okay. Give each of yourselves permission. Don't believe that the heat of the moment is the time to make everything right. Walk away. Cool off. Think things through. Focus on all that you're learning about yourself. Try to understand what's stirring within you as well as your partner. Ask yourself what the situation calls for. Empathy? Validation? Affirmation? Appreciation? Checking-In? Self-disclosure? Taking ownership of your feelings and actions? Letting go of the laundry list?

I told you at the beginning of our journey that I wanted you to have a menu of choices to choose from rather than rely upon familiar actions that sabotage your well-being. Do you see how many choices you have now? Use them! They'll serve you well. But you can't apply them effectively when you're enraged. Remember, the point of making molehills out of mountains is to embrace a process that heals the inevitable wounds that two people inflict upon one another. Use the new choices you're learning in a climate of cooperation.

Bridge-Builder's Tip

*Express your needs rather than
defend your position.*

Do you see the distinction between expressing your needs and defending your position? A position is a stance you take about something in dispute with your partner. Your needs are matters that hold importance to the well-being of you and your relationship.

Think about this for a moment. Is it safer for you to defend your position or express your needs? Which leaves you feeling more vulnerable—"I need you to be there for me" or "Here are my ideas about how and why you're never there for me"?

Defending your position is an accusation that you must prove correct. Expressing your needs is an invitation extended to your partner to join you. Defending your position is a pronouncement that your partner has failed you. Expressing your needs is a declaration of the regard that you hold for your partner.

While you furiously defend your position, any attempt to address the underlying relationship issues will have an inevitable slant to it. Focusing on your position requires that you be right and your partner be wrong. Successfully defending your position hinges on your ability to *debate* your partner rather than *understand* your partner.

Defending your position freezes you in a battle of wits where the only skills that matter are your ability to explain and justify. Can you see the inevitable harm defending your position inflicts upon your relationship? Championing your position requires you to dismiss your partner.

Can you see the paradox of attempting to resolve conflict by championing a cause? You will inevitably create more conflict than you resolve.

On the other hand, making molehills out of mountains is the end result of two people honoring each other's needs, considering the best interests of the relationship. What are the best interests of your relationship? Do these examples make sense to you? Connection. Honor. Respect. Growth. Honesty. Openness. Interdependence.

Beginning to consider the interests of your partner rather than defending your position can create an important shift between you and your partner. Selfishness will transform into sharing. Competitiveness will transform into cooperation. Antagonism will transform into mutual respect. Self-centeredness will transform into consensus building.

Here's the ultimate benefit of the shift I'm proposing. You cannot possibly begin to understand your partner while you're defending your position. Quite simply, as long as you defend your position, you'll perpetuate a log jam of ill-will. By expressing your needs and honoring the needs of your partner, you'll begin the process of tearing down the walls that have developed in your relationships.

Bridge-Builder's Tip

Identify the issue rather than focus on the problem.

Okay, you've created the appropriate climate within which to begin to resolve the relationship issues. You've taken the time to diffuse the emotional charge that exists between you and your partner. By backing away long enough to let your feelings cool off, you can come back together with the goal of creating a climate of cooperation and respect.

The next step is to make a shift in your mindset. That shift—stop defending your position. The best interests of your relationship are served by expressing your needs rather than defending your position.

Now there's one last shift to be made as you get into the substance of discussing the relationship issues. That shift is what I've been alluding to throughout this book. Shift from addressing the circumstance to discussing the underlying relationship issue. Afterall, that's what this whole exercise is about. Agreeing to focus on something beyond the circumstance that has precipitated the conflict.

Practically speaking, what that means is for you to take some time to reflect on what the underlying relationship issues are bubbling beneath the surface. I've given you an overview of the predominant themes that you can expect those issues to be. Take the time to figure out how those theme(s) may be a part of the conflict you're experiencing.

The Blueprint for Resolution

Be careful not to overwhelm your partner with a bushel basket full of issues all at once. Take the issues one at a time. You don't have to resolve all matters in ten minutes. Be considerate of your partner. Check-in with them to insure that they're up to moving on with you.

Don't be afraid to take time out. Don't be afraid to put some of the issues off until another time. Try to prioritize the issues you want to explore. At the same time, consider tackling some of the easier stuff first.

Most important of all, don't get lost in the details of the circumstances. You can always come back to figure that one out. Remember, the circumstances have been hiding the relationship problems long enough. Don't be tempted to fall back into that old habit one more time.

The last thing I want to remind you of is your commitment at the beginning of the book—let go of the familiar for something new and effective. The biggest shift of all will be shifting from trying to fix the problem to trying to resolve the relationship issue. Rest assured, with a lot of blood, sweat, and tears you can transform your unresolved issues into the foundation for your relationship's well-being.

These are important guidelines for you to follow when you begin the process of resolving your underlying relationship issues. Don't expect to follow them perfectly. Think of them more as a beacon to guide your efforts. Use them as a marker to let you know whether you've strayed too far from the target you're aiming for. If you can remain mindful of them, they won't let you down.

Hopefully, you have a better sense of what it means to pinpoint the issue and how to go about untangling the oftentimes complex issues that exist in your relationship. In the next chapter, I'm going to discuss with you some specific tools that will enable you to successfully navigate the choppy waters that get stirred up from trying to pinpoint the issue. As you become comfortable with using these tools, you'll discover that you'll be better able to stay focused on the underlying relationship issues and much less distracted by the circumstances of the conflict.

The Tools of the Trade

Relationship skills will not make your work necessarily easier, but not using them will make your journey all but impossible.

-Stanley Phillips

PART SEVEN: MAKING MOLEHILLS OUT OF MOUNTAINS

I want to share with you some tools you'll find invaluable. These tools will enable you to more effectively maintain your focus on the underlying relationship issues. A word of caution. You don't have to use all of them all of the time. Nor do you have to use any of them exactly as I've suggested that you use them.

Think of these tools as concrete ways to avoid many of the pitfalls you'll discover once you try resolving conflict the way I have suggested. Remember, our goal is to learn how to more effectively resolve conflict. The key to being effective? Put down your old ways and begin using these new ways.

As a result of using these new tools, you'll discover a new world open to you. The more comfortable you become with these new tools, the more confident you'll feel about yourself. The more confident you feel, the better able you'll be to eliminate much of the long-standing resentment and mistrust that exists in your relationships.

Imagine what it will be like for you to settle your disagreements in a manner that leaves you feeling understood by your partner. What effect will your ability to better respect and honor your partner have on their willingness to be there for you? Can you envision the day when you resolve conflict just as easily as you begin it?

You're much closer to that day than you've ever been before. You have all the ingredients necessary at your disposal. New relationship skills. The tools to implement those skills. The courage to create the necessary shifts I've suggested to you. Most important of all, the patience to see things through.

Bridge-Builder's Tool

Live in the here-and-now by resolving the unfinished business from the there-and-then.

Let's start with a global guideline applicable to all your efforts at making molehills out of mountains.

What we're trying to do is set your relationship free—free from the shackles of unresolved underlying relationship issues. Conflict that remains unresolved does one thing—it leaves your relationship shackled to the past.

You and your partner carry around the energy of all your unresolved conflict like an emotional ball and chain. The energy that I'm talking about? Hurt. Anger. Resentment. Feeling wronged. Wanting to even the score. Do you see the drain these unresolved issues create upon your relationship? How can you possibly be in the moment if you're focusing on all your yesterdays?

Very simply, you need to clean up your past in order to live in the present so that your future can be different. The path to arrive at such an end is to develop the skills that will enable your relationship to be grounded in the here-and-now rather than anchored to the events of the there-and-then.

The whole purpose of making molehills out of mountains is to resolve the disagreements from the past that continue to live and breathe in your relationships to this day. By resolving these disagreements, you can begin to

PART SEVEN: MAKING MOLEHILLS OUT OF MOUNTAINS

heal many of the wounds created throughout your relationship. You see, that's the whole reason to go through all of this work. To stop the emotional bleeding. To do away with the hurting. To undo all the ways people have of disrespecting one another.

The process of making molehills out of mountains is the means to clean up the *stuff* that gets in the way of two people caring for each other. So I ask you, are you ready to put down your weapons long enough to stop the fighting and begin the healing? Are you ready to trade in your weapons of destruction for tools of cooperation?

If you're ready to end the war, then the first thing you must do is stop living in the past. Do you get my point? Are you ready for the past to be put to bed? Are you ready to smooth off those rough edges from the past that you continually use to this day as a weapon against your partner?

You see, the choice is a simple one. Do you get more satisfaction from nursing your resentments, righting your wrongs, avenging your hurts, or healing your wounds? Isn't living in the there-and-then merely a tactic—a way of avenging the wrongs you have suffered? Although this may bring some sort of *satisfaction* to those who are so inclined, how does it help you heal the rifts that exist between you and your partner? Here's an important question for you to ponder—does reliving the past contribute to you resolving the underlying relationship issues or keeping them alive?

You see, many of us wrongly believe that the only way to heal the wounds we've experienced at the hands of our partner is by seeking revenge. But here's the truth.

The Tools of the Trade

There's only one way your wounds are going to heal. I talked about this earlier in the book. Your wounds will heal as your partner begins to understand what your experiences have been like. You can only get that acknowledgment if you're able to express what's going on with you in the moment—in the here-and-now.

Reliving in exquisite detail every crime that's been perpetrated in the past brings everything out in the open, but it does little as far as healing the wounds of the relationship. To work towards that end, you need to stop using the hurts of the past as a weapon and begin using the skills we have discussed throughout this book in the here-and-now.

You need to stop using the hurts of the past as an excuse to make your partner jump through hoops of contrition.

You need to stop using the hurts of the past as a wedge that you place between you and your partner.

What you need to do is work on the relationship as it is today.

You need to work towards creating a climate of understanding by being emotionally forthright.

You need to work towards creating common goals that will enable your relationship to grow rather than decay from the baggage of the past.

The here-and-down is a powerful balm for what ails any two people. Quite simply, the here-and-now is a bridge between the wounds of your past and the hopes for all of your tomorrows.

Bridge-Builder's Tool

Focus on behavior not personality.

Once you shift from the past to the here-and-now, there's a second shift that's necessary to make. Begin to focus on your partner's behavior rather than their personality.

Do you understand what the distinction is? Do you attack somebody for who they are or do you express how that person's behavior affects you? Do you belittle every characteristic, idiosyncrasy, way of thinking and feeling, that your partner exhibits or do you identify specific behaviors that create a problem for the two of you? Quite simply, do you believe that the formula for you getting along with your partner is predicated upon them changing *who* they are or *what* they do?

Take it from a pro, there's very little that you can do to change somebody's personality characteristics. Answer this question for yourself—just who's likely to change the essential pieces of who they are, even if they could, just because those pieces are displeasing to you?

Isn't it more likely that your partner will simply feel attacked, disapproved of, and unaccepted by you when you focus on those aspects of who they are rather than trying to understand them? And if that's true, what reaction do you think you're likely inviting?

Anger, resentment, justification, blame, defensiveness.

Now that seems pretty self-defeating, doesn't it? Focusing on your partner's personality is like pouring gasoline on a fire. It merely escalates the level of conflict you're attempting to resolve in the first place. Just remember, if your partner is busy defending themselves from your attempts to change who they are, they'll never be able to listen long enough to begin to understand where you're coming from.

Behavior on the other hand, is an easier pill to swallow. You can see that, can't you? It's less personal, although it may still sting. But more importantly, behavior is something we can more easily modify than our personality. Behavior is something we have a choice about. Behavior is an area of our life that we have more direct conscious influence over.

Although dealing with the underlying relationship issue will always sting, it will always be uncomfortable, you can more effectively make molehills out of mountains by focusing on a person's behavioral choices rather than personality. For instance, what's safer for you to hear? "When you leave the dishes in the sink for me to clean, I feel angry." Or "Why are you so lazy? Can't you stop being irresponsible long enough to think of me? You're more like a child than an adult, now get in there and clean up the kitchen."

"When you leave me out here waiting for you for a half-hour, I feel like I'm unimportant." Or "Don't you ever think of anybody but yourself? You're so selfish. How inconsiderate can you be? I'm nice enough to come down here to pick you up from work and this is the thanks I get, you ingrate!"

Do you see how focusing on a person's traits will lead

PART SEVEN: MAKING MOLEHILLS OUT OF MOUNTAINS

to defensiveness whereas focusing on somebody's behavior is less threatening?

Let's take a moment to see if you can identify how shifting the focus from personality to behavior might benefit you. Write at least three examples of how you may attempt to resolve conflict by focusing on your partner's personality rather than their behavior.

_____
_____
_____
_____
_____
_____
_____
_____
_____
_____
_____
_____
_____
_____

In order to understand how you may be sabotaging your best intentions to resolve conflict, it's important to have an appreciation for how focusing on your partner's personality affects them. Take some time and think about the following two questions. How does your partner feel in each case you listed above?

_____
_____
_____

The Tools of the Trade

Now, how does your partner react to you when they are made to feel that way?

In each example you listed, how can you shift from focusing on their personality to focusing on their behavior?

PART SEVEN: MAKING MOLEHILLS OUT OF MOUNTAINS

I trust you can see that focusing on your partner's personality is a short-sighted solution to a long-term problem. On the other hand, focusing on your partner's behavior is a long-term solution to enrich the well-being of your relationship. Living the spirit of this tip will go a long way towards relieving much of the tension in your relationship. More importantly, focusing solely on your partner's behavior will restore respect, elevate trust, and enhance the good-will between you and your partner.

Bridge-Builder's Tool

Use "I" statements rather than "You" statements.

Okay, you've got the appropriate focus, the here-and-now. You're starting to make the distinction between who your partner is and the actions your partner takes. Next, let's explore some very specific ways to talk about the conflicts that exists between you and your partner.

This tool is an important guide for how to more effectively express yourself when you're trying to focus on the underlying relationship issues. Using I statements is an important means of defusing much of the defensiveness that is present when two people are working on resolving conflict.

By using *I* statements when you express yourself to your partner, you can lessen the defensiveness in your interaction. The less defensive the two of you feel towards each other, the better able you are to *hear* each other. Creating a climate where you can *listen* rather than *defend* is a prerequisite to using any of the other skills we have discussed throughout this book.

Do you see how this tool is a fundamental ingredient for creating a climate of reconciliation? I statements are the language of taking ownership. *You* statements are the language of blame and shame. It really is that black and white. Effectively resolving conflict with your partner is predicated upon your willingness to take ownership.

It's very simple. Taking ownership means developing a better awareness of yourself. It means being aware of how your behavior affects your partner as well as being aware of how you're affected by your partner's behavior.

But taking ownership only starts with awareness. If all you are is more aware, you'll have only accomplished half of the job. The next step is expressing what you need to express. Feeling wronged by your partner is not a license to go through life as a victim. Taking ownership requires you to work things through with your partner.

So, become as aware as you can be of how you allow your emotions to rule you. When you're hurt and angry, do you take ownership of your emotions or do you disown them by blaming your partner? You see, there's that thing about choices again. Acknowledge how you're feeling or disowning those feelings by blaming your partner.

You can see the damage that disowning your feelings by blaming your partner does, can't you? Just what are the words that convey blame? It all starts with finger pointing. And verbal finger pointing always starts with, "You... On the other hand, taking ownership always starts with "I...

And you can easily see what impact either style has on your partner. "You... serves as a cue. It signals your partner to prepare to be attacked, criticized, or discounted. And when we hear that signal, we prepare to defend and counterattack. How much listening takes place in that climate? How likely is it that you're going to be heard?

On the other hand, "I... serves as a cue as well. It's a signal that you want to share something about who you are. You want to share something important about you with me. It signals that this is a time to listen to you rather than argue with you. And so, if we're of a mind to listen to you, we'll feel freer to listen rather than ready ourselves to be attacked.

We're talking about something very fundamental here. It's another one of those shifts. I'm encouraging you to shift from a posture of blame and verbal finger pointing to a posture of responsibility by taking ownership.

Blame escalates conflict. Taking ownership transforms conflict into resolution. Blame demeans both you and your partner. Taking ownership elevates the esteem of both you and your partner. Blame keeps your relationship chained to the past. Taking ownership emancipates your relationship into the here-and-now.

People look at me in disbelief when I suggest something so simple as taking ownership and communicating that ownership through the use of I statements. However I assure you that this is a very powerful formula for reducing the antagonism that creeps into anybody's relationships.

My point is simple. Your willingness to examine your part in any piece of conflict will contribute much to the well-being of your relationship. Your ability to express your ownership by communicating with the use of I statements will cement the resolution you and your partner are working so hard to create.

Bridge-Builder's Tool

Express how you're affected by your partner's behavior rather than interpret the meaning of your partner's behavior.

Here's the choice—interpreting your partner's behavior or articulating how you're affected by your partner's actions. So many relationships get swallowed up by this. I see so much damage caused by the endless time that people spend interpreting each other's behavior.

The point of making molehills out of mountains is to take ownership of how you're affected by your partner's behavior. Yet, how many keep that information to themselves?

Most people avoid expressing how they're affected by another person's actions by interpreting what motivates somebody to do something. Quite simply, they shift the focus from themselves to the other person. There's no way you can resolve any relationship issues when you continually take the focus off yourself and attack your partner.

Now, we may be adept at interpreting our partner's behavior, but it doesn't help the situation, even if our interpretation is correct. You see, interpreting another person's behavior only makes that person defensive.

I see no advantage at all in telling someone how you interpret what their behavior means. It's just like good advice. It's seldom asked for and rarely followed.

On the other hand, if we focus on what the literal behavior is, if we focus on how we are affected by that behavior, we stand a greater chance of being heard and effecting change.

For instance...

"You treat me the way you do because of the bad relationship you have with your mother. Can't you see how all the crap you dump on me is because of all the hostility that you have towards your mom? If you learned how to respect your mom, you would learn how to respect me."

Or, "I understand how upset you are. However, when you start yelling at me, I feel hurt and defensive which makes me want to lash out at you. I deserve to be treated better by you and you deserve to be treated better by me."

How effective is interpreting why somebody's angry with you (you treat me the way you do because of the bad relationship you have with your mother), as in the first example?

How effective is identifying the behavior (yelling at me), and how I am affected by it (I feel hurt and defensive)?

You always have a choice as to how you're going to address the issues in your relationship. You can choose steps that create understanding or perpetuate anger and mistrust. Interpreting somebody's reason for doing something perpetuates misunderstandings while expressing how you've been affected by somebody's behavior builds a bridge of understanding.

Bridge-Builder's Tool

Check things out.

This last step is critical to avoid the inevitable misunderstandings that arise when two people are doing the best they can to express themselves. Afterall, it's easy to understand how misunderstandings arise.

Making molehills out of mountains is very much like walking a minefield. The land mines that we need to navigate are the sensitivities that we have, the sensitivities that our partner has, and the inevitable vagaries of the spoken word.

The point I'm trying to make is that dealing with your unresolved relationship issues will challenge you to effectively communicate with your partner. There are many obstacles you need to overcome. The trickiest obstacle you will struggle with is the static created by the combined influences of your emotions and your life experiences. You see, those two influences combine to create an inherent bias as to how you choose to understand what is being said to you.

Because of this phenomena, your sincere attempts at pinpointing the issue can be undermined by the filter through which you hear what is said to you. If you can accept your fundamental vulnerability to that phenomena, then you are half-way there.

Once you recognize that you often color what's said to

The Tools of the Trade

you and done to you by your own subjective filters, you can take action to dilute the impact of your filters.

For instance, when you're confused by what your partner is doing or saying, why not get out of your head and check out with them what you're experiencing and understanding?

Or, if you're wanting to see how well you're understanding something that your partner intended to communicate, get out of your head and ask them, "This is how I understood what you just said to me—is that what you meant?"

Or, if you're familiar with the way you may distort things from time-to-time, you can become sensitized to being aware when those distortions appear. And again check-out with your partner what they are meaning by what they've said to you.

The point's a very simple one. Don't let your filters sabotage your attempt to resolve the issues that may exist between you and your partner. Be wary of the ways you interpret the events in your life. Use the simple skill of *checking things out* in order to keep your relationship grounded in the here-and-now rather than keeping it stuck in the misunderstandings created by the distortions created from your past.

Well, there you have it. Throughout this book, I have shared with you many of the tools I teach everyday in my private practice to people just like you. Some of these tools work better than others. Some of these tools suit one individual more so than others. What I can tell you with great assuredness is not what tool will work best for you, but what enables any of them to work at all.

The secret ingredient is you. Your courage. Your compassion for yourself and your partner. Your sincere desire to do the work rather than just go through the motions. Perseverance through the hard times. Understanding and kindness. You need a heavy dose of kindness to get through all of this.

The people who are most successful with these tools have only one aim in mind. They're eager to create the most loving relationships that bring honor to themselves and care and respect to their partner. For those people, to do anything less is just not acceptable.

Moving on Down the Highway

*We don't receive wisdom; we must discover
it for ourselves after a journey that no one can take
for us or spare us.*

-Marcel Proust

PART SEVEN: MAKING MOLEHILLS OUT OF MOUNTAINS

A long time ago, in the early days of my practice, I had a client say to me, "Okay, I've been in therapy for months now, yet I still have the problems I had before. How come all of these problems haven't gone away? What's the deal?"

I said, "No, you're fine. If I understand what you're saying, what you call the *problems,* will probably not go away. They're part of who you are. I mean, the difficulties and loose ends that you and I find in everyday life are part of who we are as individuals."

He looked up at me and said, "I came in here wanting you to promise me that I could stop being such an ass in my personal life. You only told me that I could be shown the problem, I never heard you say that I could find the solution. I want someone to give me a pill or something in order to make me better."

I rubbed my hands against my face and said to him, "That's not the way this deal works. I may get thrown out of town for telling you this, but, the truth is, real growth does not come from the wisdom of a psychologist, it comes from inside of you."

"Then why am I here?" he asked.

We sat there for a long moment of silence. Finally I said, "Let me tell you a story. I once worked in a hospital. Every day I would show up and do my job. I got to know the nursing staff and they got to know me.

One morning this woman with a white uniform walked around the corner. I had never met her before, so I stood up and said, "Hi, I'm Steve."

She looked at me and boomed back in a deep voice, "Yes, I understand you are the Psychologist Intern or something."

She spoke in a broken accent, I thought maybe it was Swedish. "I'm Nurse Svenson. I work for twenty years in hospital. I do my job," she said simply. Then she turned and walked away.

Over the next few days I asked other people on the ward about our Nurse Svenson and all of the responses were the same. Everyone alluded to her bedside manner as non-existent, but she was a first rate nurse.

One morning I walked into the room of a patient who was twenty years old. He had a heart defect that was only discovered two years before. Most of his life was normal, but every few months his body would fall apart and he would find himself near death.

Evidently surgery was required to address the problem. I walked into the room while Nurse Svenson was changing a dressing. I didn't want to bother them so I sat on the other bed for a moment.

"I hate this," he said. "I can't move and I can't do stuff that I like to do. Being here sucks."

"What does this mean, *sucks?*" she asked while she worked.

"You know, blows," he said.

"Blows?" she repeated.

"Yea, bites," he said. "Hey! That hurts!"

"I'm changing this dressing. Yes, it probably does hurt."

"It's all bullshit if you ask me," he said.

"You know," she said, "when I come to this country people tell me that my way of speaking was bad, but I think you are worse. You talk bad. What are you trying to say?"

"I'm trying to say that I don't like being in the hospi-

PART SEVEN: MAKING MOLEHILLS OUT OF MOUNTAINS

tal. I don't like feeling so helpless. And I don't like being poked and prodded with needles and knives. I want to be playing basketball and living my life," he said.

She worked and thought and soon replied. "I tell you something important. In my job, most people complain about being in hospital. Most people say they belong somewhere else. So listen to me now, do what I tell you—when you feel good, act like it. Then you play. When you feel sick, you belong in hospital. Because when you are sick, this is the best place for you. The only thing worse is to feel sick and act healthy."

She paused and said, "That could kill someone like you. You feel bad, get help, because you are the only one who knows how you feel."

I have a gift for understanding people, I always have. Believe me when I tell you, that was one of the most subtle yet powerful things I have ever heard anyone say.

We all are confronted with the same choices as my young friend in the hospital was. We can complain and moan about this person, that person, our boss, our lover, our family. How they don't understand us or respect us. How they don't give us what we want when we want it.

And we can make everyone else out to be the bad guy. We can stew in our hurt and anger, feeling entitled, believing that somebody else has to change.

But believe me, that's not the ticket out. The only person we have control over in this world is ourselves. We all need to learn to pay attention to how we're feeling. And when we're feeling badly, we need to have people we can turn to so that we can make our world feel safe again. That's exactly the potential that lives within each and every one of us—learning how to create relationships that support us rather than tear us down.

I don't pretend that it's easy to transform our relationships from what they are to what we would like them to be. But I absolutely assure you that it can be done.

We've been talking about the process of how to make molehills out of mountains by using a very simple skill—pinpointing the issue. But don't overlook this fundamental truism. Everything I've talked to you about in this book has a simple beginning. Everything starts with honoring yourself. Know that you *deserve* to have relationships that are emotionally safe—relationships that nurture your soul. You *can* walk away from situations that are not safe for you. At the same time, be bold enough to walk towards those relationships that will enrich your life.

But even more than that, you need to become more sensitized to your own unique levels of tolerance for the emotional intensity that's created when you build relationship-bridges. The most important thing to keep in mind is that you always have *choices* as to how you will respond when you're feeling emotionally provoked by the very human fears about getting close to another person. These fears will often disguise themselves in the conflicts that arise in your relationships. But you're slowly developing the skills to successfully unmask your fears and sensitivities.

Let me leave you with this one last thought. It bears repeating one last time. I hope these words ring in your ears as you and your partner bravely begin the process of transforming your relationship. Be kind. Have a respectful attitude towards your partner, maintain a loving attitude towards yourself. Persevere, even through the darkest moments when discouragement soaks your spirit. Rest assured that mastering the skills we have discussed in this book will enable you to navigate the sometimes rocky roads we come upon when we are building better bridges with the people who matter most.

G.B.U.

Steve

Notes

Notes

Notes

Notes

HOW TO CONTACT DR. STEVE FRISCH, PSY.D.

Dr. Frisch, Psy.D. is a clinical psychologist in private practice in Chicago, Illinois. He consults with both individuals and organizations seeking to maximize their interpersonal and professional potential.

All of Dr. Frisch's, Psy.D. programs are designed to enhance each participant's emotional and spiritual well-being. Each program participant is guided on a journey that will enable them to develop the skills necessary to create a meaningful life that expresses who that person genuinely is. This is done by developing the tools necessary to enhance the relationships one has with themselves and the people in their life.

Requests for information about these services, as well as inquiries about Dr. Frisch's, Psy.D. availability for speeches, workshops, and seminars, should be directed to Dr. Frisch, Psy.D. at the address below.

You can contact Dr. Frisch, Psy.D. at
Alive And Well Publications
826 W. Armitage
Chicago, Illinois, 60614
(773) 477-8959.

You can also contact Dr. Frisch, Psy.D. through
Alive And Well Publications' website at:
www.aliveandwellnews.com

OTHER BOOKS AVAILABLE BY DR. STEVE FRISCH, PSY.D.

Building Better Bridges:
Creating Great Relationships With the
People Who Matter Most

Moving Mountains:
Magical Choices For Empowering Your Life's Journey

Stepping Out of the Shadows
[Re]Connecting With Your Life's Journey

Making Molehills Out of Mountains:
Reclaiming Your Personal Power in Your Relationships

Stopping the Cycle of Self-Sabotage:
Making Your Relationships Safe and Fulfilling

To order Call (773) 477-8959 or write to:
Alive And Well Publications,
826 W. Armitage Chicago, IL 60614

Visit our website to order Dr. Frisch's, Psy.D. books as well as other books that focus on the mind, body, and soul at:
www.aliveandwellnews.com

The Secret To Great Relationships?

Searching for ways to make your relationships be all they can be? In *Building Better Bridges–Creating Great Relationships with the People Who Matter Most,* Dr. Frisch, Psy.D. offers powerfully simple skills for enriching your relationships. By mastering and applying these skills, anyone can create great relationships!

More than a book on creating great relationships, Dr. Frisch opens the door to a new way of thinking about how to enhance your emotional and spiritual well-being through creating great relationships. Discover for yourself the transforming powers of these relationship dynamics:

- **Enrich Your Relationships by Acceptance and Commitment**
- **Strengthen Your Relationship Bridges by Support and Trust**
- **Open Your Relationships by Effective Communication**
- **Create Involvement by Your Offering and Seeking Spirits**

If you are searching for the key to creating great relationships, *Building Better Bridges* is the choice for you.

To order by phone, call (312) 787-3412

To order by mail, send a check or money order for $12.95 plus $5.00 S&H. Illinois residents include sales tax of $1.13 per book ordered. Alive And Well Publications, 826 West Armitage, Chicago, Illinois, 60614

The Secret To Personal Empowerment?

Are you ready to transform your life today? *Moving Mountains– Magical Choices for Empowering Your Life's Journey*, provides a deceivingly simple yet powerful formula for transcending your fears in order to create a life of emotional and spiritual well-being.

Dr. Frisch, Psy.D. details remarkably powerful steps from which you can create your own blueprint for emotional and spiritual well-being. For example, Dr. Frisch writes, "To transform your life, you only need to create different choices by combining new ways of thinking and acting." The means to do so? You will learn how to:

- **Unleash the Forces of Personal Empowerment**
- **Expand Your Personal Choices**
- **Widen Your World View**
- **Master the Five Tools of Actions**

If you want to think of yourself differently, see yourself differently, carry yourself differently, and ultimately be treated differently by others, *Moving Mountains* is the perfect vehicle to get you there.

To order by phone, call (312) 787-3412
To order by mail, send a check or money order for $12.95 plus $5.00 S&H. Illinois residents include sales tax of $1.13 per book ordered. Alive And Well Publications, 826 West Armitage, Chicago, Illinois, 60614

The Secret To Transforming Your Life?

How do you create a life that reflects the essence of who you are? How do you reconnect with those parts of yourself you disowned so long ago? How do you create a life that honors your voice from within? *Stepping Out of The Shadows: [Re]Connecting with Your Life's Journey* is the perfect guide for anybody searching for the means to create a deeper sense of purpose in their lives as well as a deeper connection to the underlying forces of life.

Dr. Frisch, Psy.D. describes the process we all experience as we pursue our natural urge to grow and evolve. *Stepping Out of The Shadows* demystifies the process of enriching your emotional and spiritual well-being. You will discover how to create a personal blueprint that will enable you to:

- **Awaken Your Soul**
- **Liberate Your Spirit**
- **Illuminate Your Path**
- **Transform Your Mindset**

If you want to activate the process of healing and life transformation, *Stepping Out of The Shadows* is the perfect catalyst to begin your journey.

To order by phone, call (312) 787-3412

To order by mail, send a check or money order for $18.95 plus $5.00 S&H. Illinois residents include sales tax of $1.65 per book ordered. Alive And Well Publications, 826 West Armitage, Chicago, Illinois, 60614

The Secret of How To Love and Be Loved?

Loving relationships are created by using simple to use relationship skills that enable two people to navigate the inevitable choppy waters in any relationship. The most important relationship skill of them all? Dr. Steve Frisch, Psy.D. says that mastering the art of resolving unacknowledged, unresolved relationship issues is the single most important relationship skill of them all.

Making Molehills Out of Mountains: Reclaiming Your Personal Power in Your Relationships discusses a unique process of conflict resolution that will enable you to discover the joy of reclaiming your personal power in all of your relationships. By combining very simple to use relationship skills with a heightened self-awareness, you'll create open, caring, relationships with the people who matter most.

You'll learn how to:

- **Become as expert at resolving conflict as you are at creating it.**
- **Stop sabotaging your relationships by learning how to end your never ending patterns of conflict.**
- **Successfully resolve relationship issues rather than continually fail at fixing relationship problems.**

If you're searching for a deeper understanding of yourself and the conflicts you create in your relationships, *Making Molehills Out of Mountains* is the book for you.

To order by phone, call (312) 787-3412
To order by mail, send a check or money order for $18.95 plus $5.00 S&H. Illinois residents include sales tax of $1.65 per book ordered. Alive And Well Publications, 826 West Armitage, Chicago, Illinois, 60614

Come Visit Us on the Internet!

http://www.aliveandwellnews.com

Come see what we have for you at our web site!

- **Free newsletters** filled with information that will enrich your mind, body, and soul!

- **Free special reports** filled with information to enhance your emotional, physical, and spiritual well-being!

- **Free chapters** from Dr. Frisch's, Psy.D. collection of books and workbooks that focus on relationship bridge-building and life transformation!

- **Special offers** on our complete selection of personal growth audio tapes!

- **Special offers** on Dr Frisch's, Psy.D. books available through our web site!

- **Gift certificates** to purchase products and services from many of our contributing authors!